Palgrave Textbooks in Translating and Interpreting

Series Editors: **Gunilla Anderman** and **Margaret Rogers**, The Centre for Translation Studies, University of Surrey, UK

Palgrave Textbooks in Translating and Interpreting bring together the most important strands of thinking in a fast-developing field. Volumes in the series are designed for Masters students in Translation Studies and Interpreting, as well as for upper-level undergraduates considering a career in this area. Researchers and practitioners keen to refresh their knowledge of practice across the field will also find new material not readily accessible elsewhere. The series will include a core theory book and a number of individual volumes on specific topics covered in many MA courses.

Titles include:
Ann Corsellis
PUBLIC SERVICE INTERPRETING
The First Steps

C. K. Quah
TRANSLATION AND TECHNOLOGY

D1556659

Palgrave Textbooks on Translating and Interpreting
Series Standing Order ISBN 978-1-4039-0393-8 hardback
978-1-4039-0394-5 paperback
(*outside North America only*)

You can receive future titles in this series as they are published by placing a standing order. Please contact your bookseller or, in case of difficulty, write to us at the address below with your name and address, the title of the series and the ISBN quoted above.

Customer Services Department, Macmillan Distribution Ltd, Houndmills, Basingstoke, Hampshire RG21 6XS, England

Public Service Interpreting

The First Steps

Ann Corsellis

palgrave
macmillan

First published 2008 by
PALGRAVE MACMILLAN

Palgrave Macmillan in the UK is an imprint of Macmillan Publishers Limited, registered in England, company number 785998, of Houndmills, Basingstoke, Hampshire RG21 6XS.

Palgrave Macmillan in the US is a division of St Martin's Press LLC, 175 Fifth Avenue, New York, NY 10010.

Palgrave Macmillan is the global academic imprint of the above companies and has companies and representatives throughout the world.

Palgrave® and Macmillan® are registered trademarks in the United States, the United Kingdom, Europe and other countries.

ISBN-13: 978-1-4039-3798-8   hardback
ISBN-10: 1-4039-3798-2   hardback
ISBN-13: 978-1-4039-3799-5   paperback
ISBN-10: 1-4039-3799-0   paperback

This book is printed on paper suitable for recycling and made from fully managed and sustained forest sources. Logging, pulping and manufacturing processes are expected to conform to the environmental regulations of the country of origin.

A catalogue record for this book is available from the British Library.

Library of Congress Cataloging-in-Publication Data
Corsellis, Ann.
  Public service interpreting : the first steps/Ann Corsellis.
    p. cm.—(Palgrave textbooks in translating and interpreting)
  Includes bibliographical references and index.
  ISBN 978-1-4039-3798-8 (alk. paper)
  1. Public service interpreting.   I. Title.
P306.947.C67 2008
418'.02—dc22   2008024575

10   9   8   7   6   5   4   3   2   1
17   16   15   14   13   12   11   10   09   08

Printed and bound in Great Britain by
CPI Antony Rowe, Chippenham and Eastbourne

For my grandsons

Joseph and Oliver

Contents

Series Editors' Preface

In a world of some 6500 languages, human beings have for millennia sought to find ways of communicating across linguistic boundaries for a variety of different economic, social and other purposes. In some situations, *lingua francas* developed, for example, for trading, in others, members of one or other speech community with a knowledge of both languages interpreted the words of the other. In today's world, where migration is commonplace for economic, social and political reasons, the informality of historical practice has become unacceptable. It is in this context that the present book can be seen as a contribution to the professionalisation of interpreting (and to a lesser extent, translation) in a 'public service' – sometimes 'community' – environment, by which is commonly understood legal, medical and social services. The book is timely in its mission to outline the emergence of a profession: it is rooted in many years of experience in areas closely related to public service interpreting (PSI) ranging from the design and delivery of training courses, through the establishment and pursuit of professional codes of conduct, to political lobbying. It brings together in one place many aspects of the practice and practices of PSI distilled from this broad grassroots experience. PSI is a fast-developing area which will assume an increasingly important role in the spectrum of the language professions in the future, particularly in those parts of the world where human and civil rights are given serious consideration.

The social embeddedness of PSI practice, together with the status of its often-disadvantaged clientele, has contributed to its lack of prestige. It is often wrongly assumed by the users and commissioners of interpreters in the public services that little more is involved than a chat in two languages, whereas other forms of interpreting such as conference interpreting require years of professional training. This book sets out to correct such misperceptions by pointing out the social and personal risks of ignoring the need for trained and professionalised interpreters in the public services. Other factors, such as a reluctance to distinguish between learning the language of the host country for everyday purposes on the one hand and conducting a legally or medically critical consultation in that language on the other hand, threaten progress on a policy level. In recent discussions in the UK, for example, the costs of 'translation' have been heavily criticised in both official and popular circles. Set against this, however, are some more positive signs, such as the emergence of legally binding requirements on the use of trained interpreters in some areas and a heightened awareness among some public service professionals of access rights.

It is to be hoped that this third volume in the series Palgrave Textbooks in Translating and Interpreting will be of interest not only to PSI students but also to those undergoing further professional development, to PSI trainers, to extant or nascent professional associations, to public service employees and managers who work together with public service interpreters and, last but most certainly not least, policy makers.

Margaret Rogers
Centre for Translation Studies
Department of Languages and Translation Studies
University of Surrey
Guildford
UK

Postscript

This book was commissioned at a time when my late friend and colleague Gunilla Anderman (†2007) and I were co-editors of the Series. Gunilla asked me to take over the editing of the volume, which she had championed, early in 2007. She was convinced of the importance of a broad-ranging practice-oriented book to the development of public service interpreting and would have been delighted to see the present project come to fruition. I only regret that she was not able to do so.

Margaret Rogers
Guildford, January 2008

Acknowledgements

Developments in the public service sector are multidisciplinary collaborations. What works gets absorbed into practice. Who had what idea, when and how is rarely a matter of prime importance and often forgotten.

My primary debt therefore is to the public service interpreters and translators, to the members of the legal, health and social services and to the clients of both with whom I have worked over the past 25 years. I have also had the privilege of working with a number of civil servants committed to taking this matter forward, here in the UK and in the European Union (EU), whose contributions are often unrecognised but whose skills in analysis and development strategy have been instrumental in implementing significant changes. Members of the Chartered Institute of Linguists and of other language professional bodies have shown interest and support, irrespective of their own professional specialisms. The robust professional commitment, expertise and perception of all of them have been given generously. Their enthusiasm and good humour have kept everyone going through the inevitable highs and lows of the long development journey.

This applies not only to colleagues from the UK but also to those from other countries. These include the representatives of all the European member states involved in the four EU projects (Grotius 98/GR/131, Grotius 2001/GRP/015, JAI/2003/AGIS/048 and JLS/2006/AGIS/052) created to establish equivalent standards across the EU in legal interpreting and translation, with the hope that these would extend eventually into health and social services The five Critical Link international conferences (held in Ontario, Vancouver, Montreal, Stockholm and Sydney) have been a focal point for people from all over the world with an interest in the subject, enriched us all and promoted standards and a growing international consistency of approach.

I have sought to bring together the most significant aspects of the collective thinking and development processes while recognising the realities of limited resources, institutional reluctances and a rapidly changing context. My sources have been mainly practical activities, but a modest number of textual references are given at the end of chapters to start a thinking process, although I would encourage readers to combine reading with looking objectively at what is actually happening in their own towns. More extensive bibliographies can be found in many of the books I have referred to.

Gratitude is also due to my colleagues who have read and commented on draft chapters, and are practising public service interpreters and translators, academics or have a background in the public services. Brooke Townsley, Sabine Braun and John Corsellis have kindly commented on each chapter and others, including Jan Cambridge, Amanda Clement, Tim Connell, Emily Corsellis, Nichola Glegg, and Patrick Sedgewick have read chapters relevant to their expertise. I am also grateful to Jill Lake of Palgrave Macmillan who, as commissioning editor of the series in which this book appears, has lent her full support to the project. Nonetheless, any errors or infelicities are entirely my responsibility.

My primary editor has been the late Professor Gunilla Anderman. I am only one of many who felt bereft by her death during the completion of this text. She combined true scholarship with curiosity, charm, elegance and humour; as well as attention to detail combined with an awareness of the wider context. She insisted that I should enjoy writing this book and enabled me to do just that.

I am all the more grateful, therefore, to Professor Margaret Rogers, the series' co-editor, who took this text forward with such kindness, diligence and patience while shouldering heavy professional commitments. She applied a fresh eye and lucid intelligence to the text, and greater rigour to references and footnotes to which I confess an aversion.

Last but by no means least my thanks go to Gillian James, a former colleague of Professors Anderman and Rogers, who applied her considerable expertise gained from working on previous publications to formatting this text with fastidious attention to detail. Her good company, encouragement and sense of humour have been deeply appreciated.

ANN CORSELLIS
Cambridge, England

1
What is All this About?

In the past, the primary focus of studies of interpreting has been on communication between groups of people with different languages and cultures at an international level. The present and the future are as much about communication between people of different languages and cultures *within* national borders and concerned with the events of people's everyday lives.

The social and professional context

Globalisation and modern modes of transport have resulted in the increasing movement of people between countries for shorter or longer periods of time. People travel to other countries for work, education and pleasure. They also do so to escape natural and man-made disasters. As a consequence, most countries have multilingual, multicultural populations. In London, for example, 30 per cent of schoolchildren speak at home one of the estimated 300 languages spoken in the capital (Baker & Eversley 2000).

How that situation is handled in each country has significance for the overall national social infrastructure and cohesion. Influxes of groups of people with differing views, attitudes, perceptions and needs, who may also be in a state of anxiety and insecurity, can lead to wider repercussions. In Australia, Canada and Sweden in particular there are well-established examples of how such transitions have been skilfully dealt with, optimising the use of their multilingual resource.

This book is not about whether or not migration is a good thing or how it should be managed. It deals with one dimension of the situation found in most countries and suggests practical solutions. The dimension under discussion is how individuals and groups who do not speak the language of the country can communicate with such essential services as health care, housing, education and social services and the legal process. If, to use the London example, one third of the children in the UK capital had limited or no access to essential services, the consequences would be disadvantageous both to them and to the country. It benefits no one if a proportion of the population suffers increased infant mortality rates, miscarriages of justice, substandard housing, education and social care. It is possible to remove barriers caused by lack of language and related skills so that nurses, doctors, lawyers and so on can provide appropriate standards of expertise to individuals with whom they do not share a language, thus enabling the individuals concerned to regain control of their own affairs and become functionally self-sufficient within a new country.

There are many who may, and do, say that people should learn the language of the country in which they live. However, they often overlook the time it takes to learn a second language and the factors that affect second language acquisition (Schellekens 2001), as well as the fact that the language of medicine, the legal system and social services is often highly specialised. The ability to communicate accurately and reliably in such contexts as the police station and the doctor's consulting room requires a native speaker fluency that would be measured at postgraduate level in academic terms. Communication of that sort also demands a background understanding of the associated systems and conventions to make sense of the contexts.

The migration process is never static. In the ten to twenty years it might take for one group of other-language speakers to attain native speaker fluency in the language of their new country and understanding of its public service systems, other groups would have moved between countries, speaking another set of languages. The Gujarati speakers who arrived in Britain from East Africa some 30 years ago, and their children, now usually speak fluent English. They are generally economically stable and many are successful doctors, lawyers and business people. But since then there have been ongoing waves of migration from all over the world arising from such causes as the wars and natural disasters of the Balkans, Asia and Africa. The right to freedom of movement within the European Union also enables individuals to seek work and education in any member state. According to BBC survey in 2006 (www.bbc.co.uk/bornabroad), between 1991 and 2001, the total number of people resident in the British Isles who were born abroad, rose by 36.4 per cent, against an overall population increase of 4.03 per cent.

The reality is that nearly all countries will have to continue to deal with new arrivals, speaking perhaps yet another language and adding to

their multilingual populations. Practicalities have overtaken prepared-
ness. Uldis Ozolins from the Centre for Research and Development
in Interpreting and Translating at Deakin University in Melbourne,
described the international spectrum of response in his paper given at
the second Critical Link international conference on interpreters in the
community. He noted that Australia and Sweden were alone in having
at the outset an integrated language policy. The rest were gradually
attempting to bring together coherent systems to meet the need (Ozolins
2000).

Linguists, and in particular translators, have a tradition of acting as
catalysts for social change. The historical role of translators in spreading
'a scientific terminology, especially in medicine' (Kelly 1979:138) is a
good example of how knowledge can be transferred through translation, as also the spread of ideas from Ancient Greece through Arabic,
Latin and the European vernaculars in the medieval and Renaissance
periods (Delisle & Woodsworth 1995:124; 102–3). Indeed, vernacular
translations of the bible were often considered to have revolutionary
potential (see, for instance, Bobrick 2001). Throughout history translators and interpreters have contributed their expertise where people
who did not share a language had a need to communicate. This book is
therefore written for today's undergraduate and graduate students of
languages and related disciplines, as well as for the interested general
readers who wish to learn about developments in interpreting and
translation in the context of public services or to consider whether they
have a contribution to make to this important aspect of contemporary
social change. It is a *practical* introduction to different dimensions of
the field and is intended to provide a foundation for further detailed
study and experience. The focus is on interpreting for various public
services, but translation is also included where professionally relevant.

Sign language

Interpreting is not only a service which enables communication between
interlocutors who do not share a common spoken language; communication between a user of a particular sign language such as BSL (British
Sign Language) and a language which can be spoken (e.g. English) may
also prove impossible without a sign language interpreter who has command of both the particular sign language and the other language. Sign
languages are generally recognised as languages in their own right, with
national and regional differences such as American Sign Language and
British Sign Language. Sign language interpreting is required for those

who are deaf and need access to public services. Not all those who are deaf are users of a sign language, however; those who are deafened later in life may be more likely to communicate through trained lipspeakers or speech to text reporters[1].

Both people who were born deaf or lost their hearing as infants, and those who have been deafened later in life, find similar obstacles in gaining access to and effectively using the public services as those who do not speak the language of the country. They have common problems in such matters as acquiring adequate information about the services, how to contact them – for neither can telephone a doctor in the usual way – and how to communicate when they do get an appointment. While the principles may be the same, the specifics may have to be handled differently. For example, handcuffing deaf people who are under arrest behind their backs instead of in front deprives them of their means of communication and unnecessarily increases their distress. Interesting observations about deaf people in the legal system can be found in, for example, Brennan and Brown (1997).

Deaf communities, as very often the oldest other-language group within a dominant language community, may take the lead in new developments. As well as needing structures and mechanisms which enable them to take responsibility for control of their own lives and affairs with privacy and competence, they also need to take on their share of responsibilities to society. While these have traditionally been mainly, but not solely, concerned with their own language communities, there are considered moves towards contributions towards the wider community. For example, there is interesting work being done in Australia on the feasibility of having blind or deaf jurors[2], while in England the principle of having a thirteenth person (in the form of an interpreter) in the jury room, as opposed to twelve, is not yet explored in depth. Given the recognition of sign languages as languages in their own right and the many common principles which apply to communicating with both deaf people and other-language speakers, this book will mainly consider both together.

What public service interpreters and translators do

Public service interpreting and translation are, as the name implies, interpreting and translation carried out the in the context of the public services, where service users do not speak the majority language of the country. The term 'public service' refers mainly to those services that are provided for the public by central or local government. They include legal, health and the range of social services such as housing, education, welfare and environmental health.

The most frequently used technique in most public service interactions may be described as 'two way consecutive', whereby each speaker is interpreted for after two or three sentences or short unit of information, into and out of each language by conversational turn. Whispered interpreting (*chuchotage*) is used where occasion demands it; it is a kind of simultaneous interpreting but without the booth, with the interpreter sitting close to the listener and interpreting in a low voice as the source-language utterances are made. The most usual examples of this technique are particular stages during court hearings when the other-language speaker is not part of the exchange or where a long utterance should not be interrupted, for example, when strong emotions are being expressed. The interpreter has to know which technique would be best to use and when (see general good practice guidelines in Chapter 3). A useful glossary of terms can be found on the website of the UK-based National Centre for Languages (CILT, www.cilt.org.uk/).

One essential principle of interpreting and translation – the need for accuracy – remains the same as for any other field of operation. Whether that level of competence is always yet available in the public service sector is another matter. The difference lies in the context. In commerce and in international relations, where interpreting and translation are well established, the other preconditions necessary to conduct activities across languages and cultures are normally in place. In the public services, they are all too often not. While the businessman will conduct prior market research, the public services may not even know how many people speak which languages within their constituency. While experienced international conference delegates will know how to work effectively with interpreters and translators, the average doctor or judge will not. While the exporter, providing services across language and culture overseas, will keep a shrewd eye on advertising his product, after-sales services and quality assurance, the public services may not know how to carry out those tasks in relation to delivering their service across languages and cultures in their own region.

The first public service interpreters and translators (PSITs) therefore found themselves in the unenviable position of having to work without a functioning professional context; they were also aware that, although they might be doing their jobs properly, the public service was often not being delivered effectively. The interpreters had no support or protection and no one to turn to.

What this book is about

The delivery of a public service, such as health care or legal process, across languages and cultures is primarily the responsibility of that service. However, public service interpreters are playing an increasingly important part in the multidisciplinary efforts being made to provide overall solutions. While retaining their impartial role during work assignments, their insights into two languages and cultures and the relationships between them provide an invaluable resource in the creation of strategies to enable the delivery of an equitable and effective public service, irrespective of the language and culture of the recipient. This book therefore looks not only at the training, assessment and practice of public service interpreters, translators and bilingual practitioners but also at the wider development picture.

In Chapter 2, an account is presented of the development of PSIT in the UK, as a case study, showing how opportunities are seized on an *ad hoc* basis. Chapter 3 looks at the role and expertise of the public service interpreter, where these might differ from interpreting in other contexts and how those differences might be addressed responsibly. PSITs usually work alone. Their codes and guides to good practice have to be so thoroughly understood that they will withstand the challenges of working at speed and in such circumstances as road traffic accidents, labour wards and neighbourhood disputes. The code of conduct includes elements held in common with all interpreters such as confidentiality and impartiality. It also includes other items, such as a requirement that all rewards other than agreed payments should be graciously declined. For, while the literary translator may accept an author's or publisher's offer of dinner to discuss a text, a public service interpreter or translator would be most unwise to accept such an offer especially, for example, from anyone involved in a legal case.

The role of the public service interpreter is still under debate in some countries and contexts. Some say that public service interpreters (PSIs) should restrict their role to transferring the meaning of messages, while others would have them also give advice and opinion and take on additional tasks. Some say that PSIs should remain impartial, while others say that they should be on the side of the other-language speaker and act as advocates of their cause. This chapter explores the options and justifies the conclusions which are drawn.

Inevitably, where there are new developments there are also some differences in professional designations or 'title' between countries. Public service interpreting is called 'community interpreting and translation' in

some countries such as Australia where there is a long and distinguished tradition in this field, including established qualifications and
good practice standards. In the UK and some other countries, that title
became confused with the European Community and its languages, such
as French and German. Community interpreting also became associated
in some of those countries with a role for the 'interpreter' that was not
impartial, included a host of additional tasks and could involve training
and qualifications below the minimum level required by language professional bodies. So the title was changed to 'public service interpreter'
in those countries to denote someone who was impartial and qualified.

Chapter 4 looks at the selection, training and assessment of public
service interpreters and translators. The traditional routes of postgraduate conference interpreter training are rarely available for public service
interpreters. Trainers are faced with the challenge of training professionals who are fit to practise, within limited resources and time. The
range of languages required extends beyond those for which traditional
academic courses are offered locally. Hence, it may be difficult to source
suitably qualified individuals to be professionally trained: qualifications
in Albanian are not common in countries such as the UK, for example.

In addition, public service interpreters rarely have time to prepare for
an assignment. The man detained in the police station, the child who
has drunk an unidentified liquid and the woman in labour are not in a
position to wait until an interpreter researches the relevant terminology
and procedures. Public service interpreters have to be able to function
effectively with little warning. So knowledge of the relevant domain is
included in the training, as well as a wider knowledge of the formal and
informal terminology likely to be used. Public service interpreters also
have to respond to their work surroundings. They have to know the
geography of their localities and of hospitals and courts so that they can
reach assignments quickly, safely and on time.

Chapter 5 discusses the establishment of a professional framework. In
the public services, members of the core disciplines, such as doctors and
lawyers, belong to regulated professions. They may also have protection
of title, so that no one can call themselves a doctor or a lawyer unless
he or she has met specific requirements. Such professions arise where
trust has to be engendered because the recipient of the service is not in
a position to judge its quality at the point of delivery. That also applies
to professional linguists but only they can take the lead in establishing
their own professional structures.

A formal independent profession develops the strategies for the
implementation and protection of standards and of the code of ethics

or conduct. As yet, interpreters and translators have no protection of title but they are beginning to create professional frameworks. Without a professional body to support them, public service interpreters, for example, are vulnerable to pressure from public services to abandon their impartial status and from other-language speakers or from the media to break confidences. They would also have no protection if unsubstantiated allegations were made against them. What is more, the profession itself could become vulnerable if there were no means of bringing to book incompetent public service interpreters.

Professional structures also include the connections between the individual public service interpreters and those for whom they work. A variety of arrangements are possible and Chapter 5 concludes with a discussion of the main factors of employment.

Chapter 6 looks at bilingual practitioners, i.e. those who have a dual set of skills: language skills and the professional or vocational skills that enable them to provide their expertise in two languages without the assistance of an interpreter. Their 'other' profession, such as medicine, law or nursery nursing may not appreciate the significance and sophistication of their language skills and they need the support and encouragement of professional linguists.

Chapter 7 describes the all important training of colleagues in the public services on how to work with PSIs and across cultures so that they understand, for instance, the importance of appropriate briefings. While this training is primarily the responsibility of the discipline or service concerned, public service linguists may participate in it, and it is gradually becoming a part of mainstream in-service training. As well as participating in formal training sessions, public service interpreters inevitably find themselves tactfully performing an educational role where they find, for example, someone who has never commissioned an interpreter or translator before, by suggesting points that need to be covered in that process. It is very much in the public service ethos to promote its interdisciplinary nature and make it work.

Chapter 8 provides ideas on the policy and management skills needed to provide an organisational framework. Policy comes first: a national commitment to providing what is needed. Rightly, admiration is expressed for the South African language policy which is designed to accommodate their eleven official languages, most of them indigenous African languages not given official status during the period of apartheid. Most recognise that this policy is challenging to implement, but that does not in any way diminish its importance. Management of change requires a clear analysis of an existing situation, identification of targets and the development of practical incremental steps to cover the gap within agreed timescales. This sounds self-evident but it demands a high level of management skills to implement in an everchanging situation including some sort of organisational framework to support development.

A co-ordinated national approach is advisable because a piecemeal approach has associated risks. In the legal system, for example, to have excellent interpreting and translation facilities in courts alone, without similar standards in the police, probation and prison services, means that the courts risk trying cases on unreliable evidence gathered during the police investigation and having their sentencing options unfairly diminished. Equally, in health care services, if there is only reliable interpreting and translation in hospitals, patients may be at risk if it is not also available at other locations where health care is provided, such as the surgeries of local doctors and antenatal clinics.

In addition, in practice people's lives are not compartmentalised, so that the family which has been involved in a road traffic accident may need access to both health and legal services. The parents of a disabled child may need access to health care, education, housing and social services. There is a requirement for consistency of standards of communication across the public service sectors to produce an integrated and functional whole.

Such a national consistency presents challenges in countries where local areas have traditional autonomous administrative structures, such as in states that have a federal structure. It is something of a conceptual leap, therefore, from that to the notion of the international consistencies required to deal with the increasing movement of people between countries and the consequent requirement to deal efficiently with international co-operation and communication between legal, health and social services in different countries over individual cases and on wider matters, such as the prevention of terrorism and of trafficking in drugs and humans.

It would be unfair to face a well-meaning manager, tasked with the creation of an interpreting service for their local hospital or court, with this Pandora's Box of variables and possibilities. So this last chapter contains suggestions as to how they might go about it in a structured way.

Conclusion

The possible solutions described in this book to linguistic and cultural challenges in communication in relation to access to core public services are based on work in progress. Improvements and new ideas should evolve over time in what is surely one of the most interesting and exciting fields of professional work for interpreters, and to a lesser extent translators, and for their colleagues in other public service disciplines. There are suggestions at the end of each chapter about further reading or activities.

2
Developing Interpreting in the Public Services: A Case Study

Development processes

Historians look for facts and threads through which to measure past events and social change. It may well be that future historians, looking back at the current time, will use the degree of development of public service interpreting and translation as one of the yardsticks by which to judge how different societies adapted to the movement of people between countries in the 20th and 21st centuries. How communication channels are managed is one indicator of how societies manage change. Therefore, public services need to think carefully about what services they deliver to a multilingual constituency and how they do it.

Progress in the development of interpreting and translation in the public services is being made at three levels. There are local or regional initiatives, often started by enthusiasts, which explore new and different aspects. Nationally, individual countries are developing, often on the basis of local initiatives, strategies and systems according to their own conventions. International collaborations are developing, such as EU projects aimed at establishing equivalent standards in legal interpreting and translation in all member states. The recommendations arising from these projects have been published in Hertog (2001, 2003) and Keijzer-Lambooy & Gasille (2005). Globally, the Critical Link international conferences for interpreters in the community bring together interested participants from all over the world every four years. Started by a group in Canada with experience, expertise and commitment, these conferences have become a focus of energy. International networks and dissemination of good practice are maintained between conferences. The proceedings of those conferences have been published and reflect the growth of developments and increasing international

11

consistency (cf. Carr, Roberts, Dufour & Steyn (1997); Roberts, Carr, Abraham & Dufour (2000); Bunette, Bastin, Hemlin & Clarke (2003); Wadensjö, Englund Dimitrova & Nilsson (2007)). In 2007 the fifth Critical Link conference was held in Australia.

It is indeed interesting to note how different countries are addressing the need for public service interpreting. It could be said that the rate of progress, as in many things, is partly determined by the rate of a general growth in awareness, acceptance and understanding of migration and second language learning. In 17th- and 18th-century England, there were those who destroyed early forms of industrial machinery, such as spinning and farm machinery, because a known way of life was threatened. The transition to industrialisation was often badly handled then, but it did eventually lead to an increase in general economic prosperity. The mechanisms of social change may be better understood now, and the introduction of information technology over the last 30 or so years is an instance of what can be achieved within a relatively short time frame, given adequate information, training and a good response to needs and perceptions.

There are a variety of factors that affect the development process in public service interpreting; these are discussed in Corsellis (2003). They fall broadly into three interdependent groupings:

1. *Public services*: Do they recognise and accept the need for skilled linguistic and cultural assistance? They tend to go through a series of stages which begin with denial of any problems with communication, followed by muddling through by using the friends, family and even children of other-language speakers, or indeed anyone who might be *thought* to have some command of both languages. Finding this unsatisfactory, probably through consequent errors, they then seek *ad hoc* solutions. These are often equally unsatisfactory and include the ubiquitous coffee-stained bits of paper found pinned to the walls of police stations and doctors' surgeries which list the names and telephone numbers of people who have been helpful, such as the fish and chip shop owner who is thought to speak two languages, and the business cards of others. These people may be paid small and unpredictable amounts, but there are no clear arrangements of accountability. Some of the individuals on such lists may indeed be competent to perform the task, but there is no objective evidence to prove it. Eventually, especially where there is an increase in the number of times when help is needed and in the range of languages required, or when a very public mishap occurs, a reluctant conclusion is reached that a more systematic approach is needed.

This leads us to:

2. *Governments*: Will they see it as a priority to resource and establish national structures and systems for the provision of public service interpreters and translators with the related skill sets? From the politicians' point of view, there may be few votes to be gained out of such a venture and there will always be other things of higher priority on which to spend public money. Such a standpoint may not have so much to do with antagonism to the subject but more to do with St Augustine's prayer, 'please Lord make me virtuous, but not today'.

By comparison with the related areas of conference and business interpreting, the sums rarely add up. Most public services, such as health, social and legal services, are already operating on tight budgets. Their other-language speaking clients are rarely in a position to pay for language assistance. Private commercial companies with an interest in providing remote and face-to-face interpreting, although they may have a contribution in the right place, would have to make enormous capital investments to develop the series of skills sets at the level required so as to cover all the sectors and the necessary supportive systems on a national basis. Therefore the *national* approach is important because, for obvious reasons, there should be a national consistency in, for example, the assessments of each skill set and arrangements for engagements between interpreters, users and employees of the public service.

If the case is made to governments, and warily accepted, the spending of public funds must then be justified. This may be done through the commissioning of research to quantify any savings of public funds that can be made by engaging qualified interpreters and translators: the amount by which the quality of public services is improved and the likely value for money engendered. The involvement of language professionals in this phase is important. The outcomes of such research are likely to be inconclusive because it is ethically problematic to conduct research with experimental and control groups, for example, by comparing, say, the provision of antenatal care or court trials of similar cases to groups who had qualified language assistance and groups to whom this had been denied.

Once the initial skill sets are developed and the structures are established, a self-financing cycle may emerge whereby public services pay interpreters and translators through a budget head set aside for the purpose.

3. *Interpreters and translators*: For how long are interpreters and translators prepared to struggle on before satisfactory professional frameworks are

in place? While often willing and professional in their approach, there is a limit to what even they can do to help the public sector without a reasonable reward. It soon becomes apparent that specialised training and assessments, and professional structures, are needed to work responsibly in the public sector.

It takes time for that training, assessment and structure to be developed and established. Interpreters and translators who generously participate in initial pilot courses often do so without knowing whether they will have work afterwards or whether they will be paid for it. That can only persist for so long, and without recognition, before the government and the public services themselves feel the need to act.

The development process, therefore, involves many complexities in which interested parties from relevant public service and linguistic backgrounds are brought into a gradually widening information circle in a spiral of growth.

Developments in the UK

A formal development process started in 1983, although there were interpreters working in the public services before that time. Progress has been made through taking opportunities when they arose. Therefore, while there is an identifiable sequence of a sort, things did not necessarily happen in a coherent order, for example, interpreters were trained and qualified before there could be a proper professional framework in place for them. The result is that demand has outstripped the supply of qualified public service interpreters. Without a consistent national and cross-sectoral approach across the public services, it has not been possible to manage change and expectations satisfactorily, so that some public services, geographical areas and languages are better served than others. Only now are the threads being gathered together into a coherent system. On the other hand, without the lengthy consultative development process, it is possible that the necessary threads would not have been identified and explored in so much detail.

In 1981, two minor incidents were reported which provided the catalyst for development. The first concerned a 14-year-old French girl, who had been arrested for shoplifting while on a school trip to an English university town. The teacher and other children left the city to return to their hotel some miles away. The police officers were concerned that so young a child might have to remain in police cells overnight, especially in view of the minor nature of the matter. By chance a French-speaking police officer was found and the case taken to court that afternoon, where the chairman of the bench of magistrates also spoke French. The matter was dealt with, and the girl returned to join her class and teacher.

The second incident involved a bilingual Asian magistrate who, after hearing a case involving an interpreter working in his language, turned to the chairman of the bench and asked whether he had really intended to add to his pronouncement of sentence that the defendant must pray five times a day, as had been conveyed by the interpreter, who was a community leader.

Also in 1981, a major case in regard to interpreters emerged, although it was not reported until some years later: *R. v. Iqbal Begum (1991) 93 Criminal Appeal Reports 96*. The judgement is worth reading in full. In summary, the defendant had killed her husband by hitting him over the head with an iron bar. At her trial in 1981 she entered a plea of guilty to murder and was sentenced to life imprisonment. She spent nearly four years in prison when an appeal out of time was heard by the Court of Appeal. The basis of the appeal was that the defendant had not understood what was said at her trial; nor had she appreciated the difference between murder and manslaughter. Hence, she had not considered whether her guilty plea should, in view of her husband's conduct, have been to manslaughter rather than to murder. It transpired that the interpreter at her trial may have spoken English but did not speak the language of the defendant.

The magistrates involved in the more minor incidents mentioned above assumed that somewhere there must be a system to deal with such matters and contacted members of the Home Office, who were sympathetic but said no such system existed. The Institute of Linguists was approached, as it was and is the largest UK professional language body. The then General Secretary expressed an immediate interest because other similar enquiries had been made to him. He set up a panel including academic and practicing linguists and individuals from the Home Office and the Department of Health. The panel met regularly over the course of a year. Contacts were made, among others, with those in Australia who had developed the National Accreditation Authority for Translators and Interpreters Ltd (known in Australia as NAATI) and with those in Sweden who had had for the previous ten years, among other things, so-called work interpreters for any non-Swedish speaker in employment to communicate their rights, union rules, health and safety instructions and related matters. Colleagues in the US provided detailed information about their arrangements for Spanish speakers in court hearings. Discussions were held between members of the panel and their colleagues in the field on the situation in the UK, which revealed a patchy, uncoordinated and unsatisfactory situation. Anecdotal evidence abounded, for example, of higher incidences of infant mortality among other-language speaking groups.

The decision was then taken to do something practical. Approaches were made to the Nuffield Foundation, a private charitable trust, which granted funds to the Institute of Linguists for a part-time co-ordinator (the author Ann Corsellis) for two years in the first instance, to begin the process of finding practical solutions. It was decided that the work should, rather than cover all public services at once, begin with one area to give it focus. The legal system was chosen for a number of reasons, which included the fact that there were existing legal requirements in respect of interpreters; it was a cohesive and hierarchical system, and there were appeal systems should matters be alleged to have gone wrong.

A town was selected that had a useful, but not unusual, language pro-file. Peterborough had a long history of immigration, dating from the Romans. In 1983, its population included another large Italian popula-tion, most of whom had arrived after World War II. The original con-tingent had mainly been men, from an area of Italy devastated by war, who had been offered contracts to work in the local brick works. Their families followed. There were also Bengali speakers, Gujarati speakers both from the rural areas of Gujarat (a state in India) and those who had fled from East Africa, and a smaller number of Vietnamese and Chinese speakers among other language communities. Interestingly, over 20 years later and since the advent of freedom of movement for work between EU member states, the largest current groups of other-language speakers in the surrounding rural areas are likely to be Spanish, Portuguese and Eastern European agricultural workers. Both brick mak-ing and picking vegetables require limited knowledge of the language of the country; neither is well paid. Many of those who did and do such tasks have the qualifications to do other work, but this suffices until they learn a second language and move on to better jobs, if they stay or decide to return to their country of origin.

Transient non-English speakers added to the demand for communica-tion. Peterborough is on one of the main routes of lorry drivers (truck-ers) arriving at ferry ports in the East of England to deliver goods in other parts of the country. Those same ports are, at times, the site of criminal activities such as trafficking in drugs and humans. Peterborough is also an area where international business is conducted, and there is a modest amount of tourism and sporting events.

The preliminary work undertaken under the auspices of the Institute of Linguists involved a good deal of talking and listening. There emerged an informal steering group comprising local language teachers, members of other language communities, members of the police, court and probation services and the head of the local Commission for Racial Equality (CRE, as it was then called). In the end, much of what was achieved arose from the synergy of their different standpoints, which resulted in a collective, firm determination to achieve the necessary standards. The other-language speakers were also clear about the need for high standards. Moreover, members of the legal services were all too aware of the potential damage to the legal system and risks to their professional reputations which could be incurred if a substandard service were to be provided. Obviously, the first task was to identify what types and levels of language skills were needed. The second was to assess the existing level of language skills provided. The third was to see how to bridge the gaps between the two.

The group were fortunate in having the assistance of the late Professor Patricia Longley, a member of AIIC (the Association of International Conference Interpreters). It was clear that, without any formal training, it would be unlikely that many people living locally would have the level of skills and knowledge to meet all that was needed. She, therefore, devised a test which would not only assess existing skills but also potential abilities. Its main components were an interview, a simple non-technical interpreted role play and the translation of two non-technical texts – one into English and one into the other language. The marking sheets included the usual criteria such as accuracy and completeness. Graduate native speakers were hired to assess the non-English languages.

A public invitation was issued for people to come forward for testing, after careful explanations about the context and purpose. It was a particularly sensitive phase because the people being tested included those already working as interpreters for the legal system, those whose apparent knowledge of English had given them standing in their language communities and those whose modesty precluded them from facing up to formal objective testing. It took good diplomatic skills and much time to keep matters on an even keel, to convince those being tested that any deficiencies in language skills did not reflect on their personal worth and to cajole the modest into putting themselves forward. It says much for those who submitted to testing that they continued to support the project, whether or not their language skills were found to be appropriate.

The outcomes were perhaps predictable. In part they were dispiriting in that the accuracy of information transfer in the role plays, such as a description of a missing child, for example, was often lacking; levels of spoken and written language competence were very uneven between the two languages in question; mixing of languages was prevalent. In discussion it became clear that even for those already practising as legal interpreters, knowledge of legal terminology and procedures was often either absent or erroneous. The police inspector who sat through the testing process, including the tests of those whom he had been engaging as interpreters, was disturbed but even more determined to find solutions. There were about 16 candidates who had the makings of interpreters. The language combinations included Italian, Gujarati and Bengali with English.

The local college kindly agreed, with some help from the Nuffield funding, to host a pilot part-time course to take place for two or three hours one day a week over an academic year. Clearly, it would not be possible to have an international conference interpreter available on such a basis to teach interpreting skills. So it was decided that, for the pilots, teaching of both languages, of the legal system and translation, should take place over a year, culminating with a two-week full-time course in interpreting techniques to be taught by a conference interpreter. It was a compromise, but one which worked under the circumstances. Today, now that there are qualified and experienced public service interpreter trainers, these subjects are taught together in an integrated and much more efficient approach.

As in all the best pilot studies, the students probably taught us more than we taught them. English and the other languages, and the necessary knowledge of the legal system, were taught by experienced teachers responding sensitively to their students. The students were encouraged to assess objectively what skills were needed as well as the skills they possessed at each stage, to support one another and to tease out their own professional code and guidelines to good practice.

This collaborative approach also informed the pilot assessment at the end of the course. The Institute of Linguists Educational Trust is a nationally recognised examinations body. Consultations with students, linguists and the legal services informed the pilot examinations that were, and are, based upon real tasks and texts. The assessment tasks included interpreting role plays, translation and sight translation both ways.

There followed three successive further tranches of funding from the same source. The next phase was aimed at piloting a course for interpreting in health care. This was based in a large teaching hospital in Cambridge. The one after was aimed at the local government context that, in England, deals with a wide range of services including housing, environmental health, education welfare and social services. The original format was tested in these different areas and was found to work. Many of the same students attended all three types of courses. It was clear that one could not become qualified to work in, for example, the health care sector through a brief addition to one's training already acquired in the legal sector. They felt they needed the time and space to walk the wards and clinics, gather the terminology, understand medical processes and feel the rhythm of the communication to the same depth as they had for the legal system.

Once qualified, the interpreters needed a professional framework. They formed the Association of Community Interpreters and met about once a month to share their experiences and to update themselves through talks and discussions. The members of the public services who had been involved in the pilot courses were also invited along and participated fully in problem solving and in disseminating lessons learned among their own colleagues.

The fourth and last funded pilot phase in 1991 was for a diploma course to train trainers held at the University of Westminster over an academic year. Twelve of the best public service interpreters, with teaching potential, were selected. They came from London, the Midlands and Scotland. Sufficient funding had been raised to give them a modest salary for six months' full-time attendance, and the second six months consisted of project work, planned to be carried out at home in conjunction with their interpreting work, or teaching their own courses if these had come on stream.

The Nuffield Foundation then set up a subsequent project to promote the Institute of Linguists' model on a national basis. Funds were gathered from a variety of sources to provide tertiary colleges with modest amounts of funding, additional to what they would normally receive, to help them set up new courses leading to the assessment. Colleges were invited to submit proposals, against practical criteria, and the most likely selected. The courses were monitored carefully throughout against standards criteria by a team of people who had been involved in the pilots and whose visits were intended to give help and support as well as to evaluate such factors as selection criteria and course designs.

The outcomes formed the basis to a subsequent national approach. It has been interesting to note how these have evolved, even in a context of limited financial resources. The standard of assessment has now been raised to a level which is mapped against the National Occupational Standards for Interpreting at level 6 (approximately equivalent to honours degree level; see www.cilt.org.uk/standards); this is entitled the Diploma in Public Service Interpreting (DPSI) (www.iol.org.uk/qualifications). There are now some 20 courses leading towards the DPSI, spread throughout the UK. Inevitably, aspects of assessment have altered to accommodate over a thousand candidates a year, as opposed to the original 16 or so. For example, the original interpreting role plays were not so tightly scripted and scenarios merely sketched out to allow for individual interactions, but this, although advantageous in many ways, made consistency difficult to maintain over greater numbers of candidates and languages. There was an original fourth assessment task on professional problem solving, the code of ethics and questions about legal terminology and procedures that was partially subsumed into the other three tasks. Discussions continue as to whether a paper on professional practice might be reintroduced.

It was originally hoped that the specialist areas would be combined into one if funds became available to provide a state subsidised full-time two-year postgraduate course that would equip public service interpreters to work in any public sector context. That has not yet transpired, but many students still take more than one of the specialist options of which there are now four: Scottish law was added to English law, health care and local government. Discussions are under way to formalise Continuing Professional Development by adding assessment units for DPSI holders at higher levels or in more specialist areas, such as fraud or oncology. These would provide interpreters with a ladder for recognised professional growth and the public services and their clients with access to more experienced language skills when the occasion warranted it.

Work can never be guaranteed for public service interpreters, because no one can predict when individuals from a particular language group will become victims or alleged perpetrators of crime, be taken ill or need social services. However, the training in languages, transfer skills and knowledge of the public services, together with the students' increased self-confidence and self-knowledge, makes them better suited for other jobs in the multilingual community as well as interpreting. Among the jobs taken on by students from the pilot phases were youth work, post office management and health service administration, which normally allowed them to be available for interpreting assignments when required.

In response to the evidence of an existing uneven pattern of bilingual competence, an additional course and examination was developed in collaboration with students, teachers and the public services. This is now called the Certificate in Bilingual Skills, also offered by the Institute of Linguists Educational Trust. It is mapped at a lower level than the DPSI and is intended to assess written and spoken competence in English and another language in the general public service context at a pre-university level. The original assessment included a modest interpreting task, with a view to gauging interpreting potential, but that was dropped because some students then thought they were competent to interpret and the level was too low for professional practice. The certificate demonstrates a solid foundation for those wishing to go on to train as public service interpreters, or as bilingual public service employees such as receptionists, or indeed simply to communicate within their own communities. The last is as important as the first, and support should be given to those who wish to retain their heritage language. This lower-level course is also useful for those who may not have had the opportunity to complete their secondary education or have returned recently to education giving them confidence and the skills of learning to learn. As well as improving their language proficiency, it gives students an opportunity to explore objectively the relationships between languages and cultures.

Attempts were made to repeat the training of trainers course on a part-time basis immediately after the pilot, in order to enable attendance by those with existing professional or family commitments. This was unsuccessful at the time, perhaps because things were not sufficiently established to ensure subsequent teaching positions and make such an investment of time and energy worthwhile. Ten years later, Middlesex University established a trainers' course which is proving more popular and has been successfully repeated on an annual basis.

The embryonic Association of Community Interpreters, mentioned above, was extremely useful in giving the first batch of qualified public service interpreters the opportunity to find their feet and to explore their own practice before becoming directly involved in the mainstream of the language profession. A more robust approach, with an administrative base, was needed to take matters forward nationally. One of the last activities connected with the Nuffield Foundation was the establishment of the National Register for Public Service Interpreters (cf. Corsellis, Cambridge, Glegg & Robson 2007). This is a professional register, a not-for-profit subsidiary of the Institute of Linguists and accessible through a secure website by the public services and their approved intermediaries. It has selection criteria at various levels. Full registration requires the DPSI, or equivalent, proven hours of experience, satisfactory references and security vetting. Lower levels of registration provide a limited period of time to upgrade qualifications and experience. Re-registration is required annually. There are now some two thousand listings registered (including a minority in more than one language) in some hundred languages with English. Registrants may also belong, if they choose, to professional language bodies. This structure may transmogrify as matters develop.

The parallel set of skills needed by public service personnel to work with interpreters and across cultures was developed during a year's work with a large probation service: this was useful because probation involves the approaches of both the formal legal work and the more informal social support activities. These are set out in Chapter 6 and were deliberately designed so that they can be adopted by and adapted to any public service.

Perhaps because the legal services led the pilot scheme, their arrangements are ahead of those of health care and local government services; or perhaps this is due to more specific legal requirements about interpreting and translation. There is a National Agreement on the Arrangements for the Attendance of Interpreters in Investigations and Proceedings within the Criminal Justice System (2002). This has been revised under the auspices of the Home Office as the Agreement on Arrangements for the Use of Interpreters and can be consulted on the Home Office Police website (http://police.homeoffice.gov.uk/ news-and-publications/publication/operational-policing/national-agreement-interpret.pdf). It is intended that it will have an accompanying series of good practice guidelines on the staff intranets of the various legal services. It is hoped that these arrangements might roll over into other sectors, such as health care, local government-related services and the Department of Work and Pensions, all of which currently have less well-developed PSIT systems.

So, training courses, examinations and registration processes have been developed, piloted and established. There remain to be put in place national formal systems to support interpreters in their day-to-day professional lives as well as the intermediary structures through which public service interpreters might be employed. This includes national guidelines for situations where public services choose to outsource these arrangements rather than engage people directly through the Register. In the Netherlands, a system of government-funded regional interpreting and translation centres had been established, although this is currently being re-thought (cf. van der Vlis 2003). There are increasing numbers of commercial agencies, some very large, operating in many countries. They can be variable in the standards and content of their delivery.

The principles of establishing a professional framework are explored in Chapter 5, but the practical implementation is yet to be completed on a nationally consistent basis in the UK. The notion of a nationally agreed, annually reviewed scale of fees, terms and conditions is being debated. Those rates should apply, whether or not the arrangements have been outsourced to intermediary agencies. A specified minimum rate gives some protection to the interpreters, gives clear guidelines to public service managers and avoids any infelicitous haggling. Systems to give support, mentoring, supervision and in-service training are gradually emerging in some areas but are yet to be disseminated nationally.

National arrangements are necessary because, by definition, interpreters and translators can be called to assignments anywhere in the country where they might be needed. It is sensible, therefore, to have consistent systems and processes throughout the country so that PSITs can operate under more or less the same arrangements wherever they find themselves. Consistency between public services is equally important. At the moment, because the legal services are better organised and offer better fees, a disproportionate number of registered interpreters understandably specialise in the legal system.

In the next chapter we go on to consider in greater detail the role of interpreters and translators in the public services.

Suggested further reading

Garzone, G. and Viezzi, M. (eds) (2002) *Interpreting in the 21st Century: Challenges and Opportunities*. Amsterdam: John Benjamins.

Hale, S. (2004) *The Discourse of Court Interpreting: Discourse Practices of the Law, the Witness and the Interpreter*. Amsterdam: John Benjamins.

Mason, I. (ed.) (1999) *Dialogue Interpreting*. Special issue of *The Translator* 5:2. Manchester: St Jerome.

Mason, I. (ed.) (2001) *Triadic Exchanges. Studies in Dialogue Interpreting*. Manchester: St Jerome.

Mikkelson, H. (2000) *Introduction to Court Interpreting*. Manchester: St Jerome.

Pöchhacker, F. and Shlesinger, M. (eds) (2005) *Healthcare Interpreting: Discourse and Interaction*. Special issue of *Interpreting* 7:2. Amsterdam: John Benjamins (also available as Pöchhacker, F. and Shlesinger M. (eds) (2007) *Healthcare Interpreting: Discourse and Interaction*. Amsterdam/Philadelphia: John Benjamins.

3

The Expertise and Role of Public Service Interpreters and Translators

Interpreters

There are still those who would encourage the use of children as interpreters, on the grounds that it improves the children's language skills and that their family members will trust them more than qualified interpreters. To a responsible professional this approach is untenable because they appreciate that the core role of public service interpreters and the linguistic and cultural expertise they need to fulfil it are exactly the same as that of interpreters in any other field. Any differences between public service interpreters and interpreters working in other fields lie mainly in the following:

(i) domains – the subject of assignments
(ii) physical surroundings
(iii) participants involved in a communication exchange
(iv) codes of conduct and good practice guidelines

(i) Domains

As indicated in previous chapters, relevant domains for PSITs include legal, health care and the range of services that come under the auspices of local government, such as housing, education welfare, environmental health and social services.

There are three obvious demands on interpreting arising from the situations in which interpreters work in the public services. The first is the need to work bilaterally, that is, both into and out of the two languages concerned. It would not be feasible, for example, for a French visitor to have two interpreters to assist her when she visits her doctor: one to work into English and one into French. The challenge for public service interpreters is that they must keep up to date with both their working languages and in a range of formal and informal registers and language varieties. In addition, while native speaker competence might not be expected in a second language, pronunciation and intonation must be easily understood in both languages.

The second demand on PSIs is the lack of time often available to prepare for an assignment. A person trapped in an overturned lorry, a woman in labour or a domestic dispute cannot be put on hold until the interpreter researches the topic and consults dictionaries. Therefore public service interpreters are trained to have a sound background understanding of the structures, procedures and processes of the relevant services, as well as a grasp in both languages of the registers likely to be used and the associated formal and informal terminology. They develop information retrieval skills that allow them to build on their existing knowledge during and between assignments so that normally less has to be done immediately prior to an assignment to equip them for the immediate task ahead. They also collect a range of useful sources that can be accessed at short notice.

Last, but not least, is the issue of facilities where there is a need to employ simultaneous interpreting, such as in courts, child protection conferences and public meetings: there are very rarely any booths to interpret from. Some major courts may acquire them, and the concept of portable headphone systems is now beginning to be considered because they would be particularly useful on occasions where there are more than one other-language speakers. Therefore the normal interpreting techniques employed are 'two-way consecutive', which can be understood as interpreting for each speaker in turn where a turn is two or three sentences, or, in appropriate circumstances, whispered simultaneous or *chuchotage* where the interpreter sits next to the listener and whispers the interpretation at the same time as the other interlocutor is speaking. The interpreter has to know which technique would be best to use and when (see general good practice guidelines later in this chapter).

(ii) Physical surroundings

Interpreters who work in international or commercial settings will usually do so in interpreting booths or offices with forays into meetings, social events or tours of business premises. The physical surroundings of public service interpreters can be very variable and are largely unpredictable.

Public service interpreters are sometimes tempted to regale other linguists with descriptions of assignments that involve aspects of high drama and excitement, in the same way as lawyers share their most vivid cases and surgeons their most spectacular operations. The reality is that a working week will normally largely consist of routine work in hospital outpatients' clinics, police stations, courts, benefits offices, school parents' evenings, immigration offices and social housing departments. Nonetheless, what is routine to the professionals can be very significant to the other-language speakers involved and professional interpreters will seek to maintain the same high standards whether they are dealing with parking tickets or serious fraud; with a child's worries about a playground bully or with charges of child abuse.

Some assignments require that the interpreter knows and follows specific protocols. When working in prisons, for example, there are procedures to be followed for security purposes in most countries and, indeed, for the safety of the interpreters. Trained PSIs know which of their possessions they may take inside a prison and which to leave at the security gates. They also know not to make telephone calls on behalf of prisoners, however apparently innocent. Neither do they take anything to or from the prisoner without permission.

A working week may also bring midnight calls to hospitals, to police cells and to the hard shoulder of a motorway where there has been an accident involving one or more speakers of other languages. It can also on rare occasions bring calls to major incidents such as bombings at underground stations, airport accidents and terrorist situations.

Training can only go so far to prepare interpreters for any situation. Experience and the support and advice of senior and more seasoned colleagues provide the rest. As so often, it is the simple preparations that make the difference between a professional and non-professional approach over and above actual interpreting competence; this is perhaps best illustrated through the following three practical examples.

Quite rightly, conference and business interpreters dress to match their work situations and clients. Public service interpreters soon learn that, while they have to preserve a professional formality in what they wear, this has to be combined with comfort, appropriateness and serviceability. For example, patients and detained drunks may vomit and have poor personal hygiene. Weather and temperatures can change over the space of a few hours and professional appearance has to be sustained at all times. Washability, dignity and comfort are the watchwords.

The perceptions of appearance by the other parties should be taken into account. Public service interpreters are very visible to all involved but should not stand out. Public service professional colleagues – such as doctors or lawyers – will expect interpreters, as fellow professionals, to dress in a manner similar to their own. Men should normally wear suits and ties in countries where they are worn and women formal dress. The equivalent national dress, such as saris, is of course acceptable. The other-language speakers have also to be taken into consideration by dressing in a way which is sensitive to the situation. The neatness of dress adopted by the professionals offering them a service denotes respect for them, although it must never be seen as trying to be superior.

The second practical example is the interpreter's bag/rucksack. It is normally kept ready and replenished for a speedy departure, next to a securely fixed notepad where the interpreter can leave a message and contact number to tell colleagues or family members where they are. The bags themselves are serviceable, waterproof and securable because they have to see long service and protect the contents from the weather and loss. Most are either flat-bottomed shoulder bags or rucksacks with a top opening for easy access so that they can be easily carried and not mislaid, particularly in situations that involve a plethora of people and equipment or where an unattended bag could be thought to constitute a security threat. The reality is that there is rarely any place for the interpreter to store their belongings. They need their bags by them anyway and should be able to take them from place to place when, for example, following an other-language speaking patient from ambulance to accident and emergency department, then to X-ray department and then to the ward.

Contents of the bag vary according to the individual, but are selected to see the interpreter through a working day or night that may be of unpredictable length. They are likely to contain such items as: charged mobile phone, note book and pens, small dictionaries and/or personal glossaries, identification badge, personal logbooks where these are used to record assignments for registration and training purposes, maps, torch, tissues, small toilet kit, book to pass any waiting time, any personal medication or even just throat pastilles, spare clean clothes such as a shirt blouse, spare sweater and umbrella, water bottle, fruit bar, spare car and house keys, emergency cash for transport or a snack. Some interpreters attach a label inside with a checklist to remind them of what must be done if they have to leave home or office in a hurry.

The third example relates to health and safety. In most circumstances such considerations would not apply but working interpreters should be alert to situations where they might, and act responsibly towards themselves and others. A properly organised training course is likely to include a session on health and safety. Colleagues in other professional disciplines will have had more extensive training on the subject, relevant to their own tasks, and are likely to watch out for the interpreter.

However, one often learns more from experience, and from watching others, than in the classroom. There are two obvious dangers for PSIs. One can be the risk of physical violence from, for example, people who are experiencing mental health problems, are not sober or are just very angry. It is wise for interpreters never to allow themselves to be left alone with a client where such circumstances might arise. It is sensible, when accompanying officers on a drugs raid for example, for the interpreter to ask for a knife-proof jacket if the police officers are wearing them. Secondly, there are methods commonly used by public sector staff for guarding against infections such as AIDS.

There are usually clear public service procedures designed to deal with these matters. It is fully acceptable for interpreters to discuss potential risks in advance and to seek advice on how to handle them, remembering that if they do not follow such procedures they may be putting themselves and others in a difficult position should things go wrong. These procedures include systems for identifying the signs of potential risks, avoiding such situations and practical solutions such as knowing where alarm buttons are in each building. In view of the inevitable ongoing change in protocols, it can be helpful to have a system whereby relevant information on this subject can be passed on to colleagues, in a form of wording agreed with the relevant public service to ensure accuracy and to avoid endangering security arrangements.

Potential risks of inappropriate intrusions into interpreters' personal privacy, and of harm to them, outside the workplace are fairly unusual but care should be taken to minimise the risk. Many interpreters live in small shared language communities where everyone knows who they are and where they live, in the same way as people in villages and smaller towns are likely to know where their doctor, police officer and social worker live. Strategies and conventions, similar to those applying to other professions, have to be developed so that interpreters are not inappropriately bombarded with requests for explanations of such matters as how to fill in a form at home or whenever they go shopping – any more than one would approach a doctor in a supermarket to discuss ailments. This means, of course, that workable alternatives should be available in the same way that patients know the appropriate places and times to seek medical help.

In the relatively rare circumstances where there may be a significant risk to the interpreters' own security, interpreters may be brought in from another locality and their names withheld from other-language speaking clients. They can simply be addressed as Mr/Mrs/Ms Interpreter. Some interpreters consider taking out personal injury insurance along with professional indemnity. Any threats should be reported immediately to the authorities. This having been said, a sense of proportion has to be retained because interpreters probably face no higher risks than anyone else working in the public service context.

(iii) Participants involved in a communication exchange

Interpreters working in other fields often work with people who speak the standard variety of their language, share a basic common understanding of the context such as a manufacturing industry or international monetary policies and are not frightened, anxious or at risk of losing their life, liberty or quality of life.

This is often not the case for public service interpreters. Either the public service practitioner or the other-language speaker may have a strong regional accent or dialect and express themselves in a range of formal and informal registers. Interpreting in a dispute on fishing catches between officials from the North East of England and German trawler captains from Hamburg may require not only an appreciation of fishing tackle and deep-sea fishing but also a grasp of non-standard varieties of English and German. Other-language speakers who are resident in the country may, on occasion, speak the version of the language they arrived with over twenty years ago, which has fossilised. There may also be some language mix and shift among the second generation.

There may also be imbalances of power to be addressed, arising from the amount of shared knowledge. In the dispute on fishing tackle, as an example, both parties share a common level of knowledge of the subject. However, a patient will not share a common level of medical knowledge with a doctor, an individual is unlikely to have the same level of knowledge of the law as the lawyer he or she is consulting and the parent going to visit a teacher may not know much about the country's education system. They may all be anxious. The public service personnel may also be anxious because they do not have the knowledge of the other-language speaker's needs, perceptions and attitudes that they need in order to do their jobs properly. It can be stressful for them too because they are at risk if they make decisions based upon inaccurate information. They also have time management problems in having to get through their work within a defined time schedule. That is often stretched when the fates decree that the moment when an other-language speaker arrives to seek help in a police station or accident department coincides with the arrival of six fighting drunks and a road traffic accident.

There are therefore disparities between the other-language speaker and the public service personnel in terms of shared common knowledge of the topic, of each other and of the context of the service. Neither may be sure how to manage their relationship in the ways they would like. Both might be nervous and unsure how to proceed.

(iv) Codes of conduct and good practice guidelines

All of the above has to be managed so as to maximise reliable communication and service delivery, to minimise risk and to increase energy and cost-effectiveness. How that might be done is emerging through the codes of conduct and the guidelines to good practice which are being developed in the light of experience. In order to be credible and effective, codes and guidelines should, through the auspices of a national professional language body or register, be nationally consistent, transparent and publicly understood.

A professional language body or register is there not only to implement but also to protect the codes and guidelines. Individual interpreters and translators may, for example, need backing to stand by their codes in the face of powerful pressures when others find those codes inconvenient. There is anecdotal evidence of pressures being brought to bear on interpreters to break confidentiality, to act partially and even of judges becoming angry with interpreters who decline an assignment that the interpreter considers to be beyond their expertise to carry out competently.

The code of ethics or conduct sets out the core standards of professional behaviour. These are timeless, transparent and encapsulate core principles. The guidelines to good practice are the procedures that should be used to support the implementation of the code. These guidelines should be followed whenever possible but it is accepted that, on occasion, practicalities might intervene. For example, the guidelines may suggest a protocol for introductions between interlocutors (see below: General guidelines to interpreting good practice) but it may be best to omit that until later if a patient is haemorrhaging badly. There are general guidelines that cover most eventualities and guidelines for specific purposes that go into more detail, for instance, on how witness statements should be taken in police stations. However, where there are allegations of a breach of the code, disciplinary panels (see Chapter 5) will take into account whether the guidelines to good practice were followed on a particular occasion and, if not, the reasons why.

Professional codes and guidelines are not unlike Highway Codes which, if they are understood and followed, prevent accidents. As with the Highway Code, where it is essential that everyone follow the same code; consistency is imperative. In the same way it is also important for all road users to have a background understanding of each other's codes, so that bicyclists or motorists can predict what lorry drivers might do; so it is that all public service disciplines need to have an appreciation of each other's codes.

The principle underlying each element of the code for public service interpreters is similar to the codes of other public service professions and, indeed, other branches of the language professions. Confidentiality, for example, is common to all. Where there is more of a divergence, it is in the guidelines to good practice which are designed to support the implementation of the code within specific contexts of public service interpreting.

The codes and good practice guidelines of the public service personnel themselves should complement those of the interpreters (see Chapter 7). For example, the public service staff commissioning an interpreter should observe the good practice which complements the interpreters' good practice in accepting an assignment (see also below: Key points in a code of practice).

There is still debate over some aspects of codes and good practice guidelines. A consistent national, and even international, approach would be desirable so that, like interpreters in other fields, public service interpreters can work in the countries of both their languages. We return in more detail to the important topic of a code of practice below, following some comments on the role of translators in public service contexts.

The need for translation in the public services

The standard of translation skills and good practice required in the public service sector is no less than is required in other contexts, regardless of text length. The few lines that comprise an operation consent form, for example, are of profound significance to the person who agrees to their content, and accuracy is therefore paramount.

It may be that texts are not seen as 'important' as an operation consent form but they have truly important implications. A good example of this is where children are left to translate their own school reports for their parents, who do not read the language in which the reports are written. The children may understandably be tempted to offer a glowing account of their achievements, which is not accurate, if only because of the pressures to succeed at school for the children of new arrivals. Written messages sent to school by the parents via the child may also be inaccurate. The reasons for those pressures are among those that require teachers and parents to be able to communicate with each other and to be mutually supportive for the sake of the child, in a situation that may not be easy for any of them. Otherwise, a number of things may happen. Firstly, the child is put in a position of power that distorts the family dynamics; secondly, the parents lose the power to exercise their responsibilities through lack of information; thirdly, the teacher may not receive relevant information about the family situation and life events and, last but not least, the children may lose out.

There are few public services that do not involve the written word. Texts include forms and notifications, letters, reports, information leaflets, transcripts of covert surveillance recordings and parking tickets. Not having access to information about voting rights or mundane activities such as refuse collection, or not being in a position to complete tax forms, applications for driving licences and so forth can be serious obstacles to conducting one's affairs on a day-to-day basis. When other-language speakers get into situations that involve health care, legal and social services, the need for accurate and reliable translation becomes even more vital. Providing translations for vital written documents is just as much a factor in ensuring access to public services as interpreting, as already recognised by some agencies such as the Vera Institute of Justice in the United States (for instance, *Translating Justice: A Guide for New York City's Justice and Public Safety Agencies to Improve Access for Residents with Limited English Proficiency* (2005)).

Translation in the public service sector can also include an international dimension. In the legal system, individual cases can involve more than one country and there is increasing mutual recognition of evidence, judicial decisions and arrangements for bail. International co-operation on the part of criminal justice systems is required for such matters as the prevention of terrorism and trafficking in people and drugs. Exchange of medical reports between countries is not uncommon. In cases of contested custody of children living in another country, sensitive assessments may be made by social workers in both the countries involved.

Public service interpreters are normally trained and assessed to translate short informational texts into and out of both their languages. Unless they have additional translation qualifications, they should refer any longer, complex or technical texts to a qualified legal or medical translator, for example. This is confirmed by their obligation to abide by their code of practice that includes a duty to admit professional limitations. Professionally trained interpreters recognise that translation involves a different skill set to their own – and *vice versa*.

Much translation work in this context appears unglamorous but its absence, even in apparently small events, can have serious consequences.

Good illustrations of this are medication labels and instructions. The translation of the labels on medications, setting out the name of the medication, how much is to be taken, how and when, is essential. Firstly, even with the intervention of interpreters and bilingual staff during the medical consultation, patients and carers sometimes do not remember accurately what was said to them in a doctor's surgery, in any language. They need to have instructions they can read and refer to at home.

Secondly, precision is essential in finding accurate equivalents, and relevant descriptions, not only for the name of the medication where available but also for terms concerning its administration to ensure a reliable compliance based on understanding. Does, for example, the instruction 'take four times day before meals' refer to the fact that the medication absorbs better when taken before eating, that it eases digestion or that it should be taken at regularly spaced intervals throughout the day? The translator therefore needs to understand the thinking behind the original instruction and to take this, as well as any technical terminology, into account, for example, in relation to eating customs in the target culture. Icons could be considered, as an addition, where there are problems with literacy.

Thirdly, the effective provision of translations – especially translations of short texts such as this – is a matter of management. It would be both expensive and cumbersome for a qualified translator to be located and commissioned to translate one label. In countries where labels for medication are printed by computer in pharmacies, it should not be difficult to provide an option to produce labels in relevant languages as well as the majority language, stating the dosage and method of administration. The cost of providing translated leaflets to accompany medication that explain its purpose and content and possible side effects could well be outweighed by the cost of potential misadministration.

Translators working in the public sector

The qualified professional translator is likely to possess the core language skills and translation competence to work in the public services. The professional context may come as something of a surprise to them if they have been working in commercial or international situations. The main differences they will have to accommodate are that:

- public service personnel are often unfamiliar with procedures for engaging with and commissioning a translator; they may also not understand what the translation process consists of;

- few countries have created structures and systems in the public sector to organise the translations they need;
- budgets may not have been set aside for the purpose.

Ideally, all three issues would have been addressed through national and/ or professional policy and implementation. Given that they probably have not, translators will find it easier to do what they can to contribute to worthwhile long-term solutions and to deal with the short-term by tactfully educating public service colleagues through interdisciplinary collaboration. Suggestions on the engagement of translators and guidelines for working with them are included in Chapter 7.

Key points in a code of conduct

What follows is not in any particular order of importance. It begins by looking at the relatively non-contentious items in most codes of conduct (lettered items in bold) and examples from the guidelines that underpin them. The latter are designed to illustrate how codes can be implemented in the real world, which can be unpredictable and throw up professional ethical dilemmas on a fairly regular basis.

Interpreters and translators should:

(a)   **only accept assignments which they deem themselves competent to carry out to a satisfactory standard**

(b)   **disclose any professional limitations which may arise during an assignment and take steps to remedy them or withdraw**

(c)   **declare any conflict of interest arising from an assignment**

The way in which interpreters actually accept an assignment is important, if only because the public service employee contacting them may not have commissioned an interpreter before or been trained to do so properly (as described in Chapter 7). In real life, those who have commissioned an interpreter may go off duty and forget to write things down or to pass on information. The following discussion goes into some detail but the process need not in fact take long and some interpreters keep a checklist in their diary or a notebook to fill in as an *aide memoire*.

When initially contacted, interpreters will first determine, in the normal way, whether or not they are available on the date and at the times required. They will then proceed to ask the name of the other-language speaker to determine whether any conflict of interest might arise because they are related to that individual or know them to an extent where their impartiality might be, or be perceived as being, at risk. It may be that the other-language speaker and the interpreter do know of one another, as suggested earlier in this chapter. The interpreter should declare this immediately and seek informed agreement from both the other-language speaker and public service personnel as to whether it is acceptable to proceed on this basis. It may be that the other-language speaker wishes to discuss very private domestic matters and would simply feel uncomfortable doing so with the help of an interpreter they may see around on a regular basis, although that can partly be overcome by the confidentiality culture and professional trust discussed later in this chapter.

Language matching is the next important item. Public service personnel, such as police officers and nurses, cannot be expected to be experts in language identification. They may have got as far as identifying what they think is a language such as 'Chinese' or 'Indian', unaware that many languages or dialects are spoken in those countries. A case is reported in Chapter 7 (*Regina* v. *Endenico Belo*) where mismatching led to legal problems. If in any doubt, then a short telephone conversation with the other-language-or dialect-speaker may be needed to confirm a language match. In certain circumstances, such as when those suspected of serious offences are being held in a police station, the conversation should be conducted under the supervision of an officer and perhaps recorded, to avoid any possible future claims that security was breached.

Then enquiries are made about the topic of the assignment, and whether unfamiliar or unusual procedures are anticipated. It is at this point that interpreters make a judgement as to their competence for the task. A matter of shoplifting chocolates from the supermarket is likely to be straightforward for an interpreter already trained in the relevant procedures. However, allegations of defects in the internal workings of a lorry may need some thirty minutes' preparatory work by the interpreter on the terminology relevant to brake mechanisms and so forth. This can often be done through reference to a dictionary or a short telephone conversation with a colleague or a mechanic.

A court hearing involving the testimony of expert witnesses about ballistics or a medical condition could need longer preparation, and the interpreter has to gauge whether they have the time and opportunity to do this before the hearing, if the subject is not already within their expertise. Interpreters should also have the facility, under appropriate security arrangements, to see relevant documents before and during a trial. A lengthy contested high court hearing on a matter of complex company fraud will best be given to an interpreter with experience in the subject. Fortunately, many public service interpreters are part-time and have other qualifications in other subjects. Clearly an interpreter with knowledge of accountancy would be best equipped to deal with the case of fraud.

One of the first rules for any profession is 'to know when you don't know'. Admission of professional limitation is well recognised and respected across all disciplines and no one should think worse of an interpreter who admits to being not sufficiently familiar with a topic. Public service colleagues can, once trust is established, be helpful in briefing interpreters. Texts to be used or consulted during an assignment can be made available, under appropriate security arrangements, for the interpreter to digest in advance. It would be unacceptable for interpreters to accept assignments, which they knew they were not competent to perform adequately.

It is also perfectly acceptable for an interpreter to admit to professional limitations *during* an assignment. It may happen that an interpreter does not recognise a name, but finds that he or she knows an other-language speaker on arrival at the assignment. That fact should then be declared and discussed at the outset. It often happens too that, while the topic was rightly judged to be within an interpreter's competence at the outset, a word or phrase may arise during an assignment that the interpreter is unable to deal with. That should be admitted at once, in a suitable way, and clarification sought. Maybe unfamiliar terminology crops up or new procedures are mentioned; maybe there is a moment of lexical amnesia – which can happen to the most experienced – or maybe a speaker expresses himself or herself ambiguously. Muddling along in hope can undermine the whole communication process very quickly. As in communication in other contexts, units of information exchange are built up in a process not unlike building towers of bricks, and if one brick is unsound, the integrity of the rest is put at risk. Equally, an unforeseen conflict of interest might arise during the assignment such as if a relative of the interpreter turns up as a lawyer or as a judge in a legal case or it turns out that the interpreter or a relative has an interest in a company that emerges as being part of a discussion. As in other disciplines, if professional limitations or conflicts of interest cannot be resolved satisfactorily and transparently, the interpreter should withdraw from the assignment.

Emergencies are a different matter. If the interpreter is, for example, the only person available at short notice with the requisite language combination needed, he or she would do their best in such an assignment while making clear their predicted limitations to all parties involved at the out-set, and preferably in writing if at all feasible. All possible strategies should be employed to ensure accuracy.

Before accepting an assignment, interpreters need to clarify travel arrangements and the location of the assignment. This may include parking arrangements, if they have their own transport, and, if they do not, whether and how that place can be reached and left safely, particularly at night. Many hospitals, courts, police station and local authority buildings have security systems these days, which have to be negotiated. No interpreter wishes to be circling a building looking for a parking space or not being able to get in when they eventually arrive. Sensible security considerations will normally mean that interpreters will not arrange to meet their public service colleagues in a non-official venue, particularly after dark, but arrange to meet up with them at, for example, a police station or hospital. The name, whereabouts and contact number of the person the interpreter is to report to should be ascertained together with the file number of the case for identification purposes in case, for example, of unforeseen delays.

Last, but not least, the agreements over fees, expenses and such like (as described in Chapter 5) should be completed before the assignment, preferably in writing. It may be, however, that there are existing agreements in place with the public service or an agency which covers the assignment in question.

(d) **Interpreters and translators shall not delegate assignments, or accept delegated assignments, without the consent of the parties concerned**

If arrangements are more informal, serious risks can be run on the occasions when interpreters, having accepted an assignment, are prevented from meeting their obligations or find better things to do, passing the work on to someone else. That someone else may or may not be competent to do the job. In such circumstances, there may be little recognition, outside the language profession, of the level and type of skills needed, any fees are often nugatory and there is a sense that anyone with some (undefined) language skills is doing a favour by 'helping out'.

There are fewer contexts nowadays where it can be said that people are not aware of the skills needed. The fact that those skills may not always be available is a different matter. There are conference interpreters who say they would not accept assignments in the public service context because they do not feel equipped to do so; they would be professionally reluctant to interpret, except in an emergency, where they do not have a grasp of the terminology or procedures.

Like all professionals, public service interpreters must honour any assignment they have agreed to undertake. If, as can happen, they or members of their family are taken ill or another assignment has over-run, they must contact the principal who commissioned them at once. If the commissioner is an agency, the agency should be in a position to replace the original interpreter with another of equal competence and inform the relevant public service accordingly. If the interpreter has been commissioned directly by the public service, a nurse or lawyer might well then ask the interpreter who else could do the job. This is one of the many times where professional registers, such as the UK National Registers (www.nrpsi.org.uk), of trained and assessed inter-preters are relevant because the nurse or lawyer can simply be referred back to the register. Where there is no register, matters are more prob-lematic. The interpreter may suggest suitably qualified colleagues but the onus for selecting and commissioning them lies squarely with the public service.

It may be that the nurse or lawyer who has not been trained in such matters does not know what the criteria for selecting an interpreter might be. Where no such training has been given, public service inter-preters often find themselves educating colleagues in other disciplines, and will have to explain what is required. Otherwise, for the sake of expediency and with the best of intentions, the nurse or lawyer might simply call upon the services of the obliging local Chinese restaurant owner or the kind cleaner with unproven second language skills. These individuals may or may not have the requisite level of bilingual language skills. Many new arrivals working in the catering or cleaning trades are graduates of universities in their own countries and are diligently learn-ing the language of their new country. They are, however, unlikely to be adequate to the task and it could be unfair to put them in that position. If there is nevertheless absolutely no feasible short-term alternative in emergency situations, the nurse or lawyer should be in a position to appreciate the essentials of using an untrained person, and be fully aware of the risks and how to mitigate them. There is a salutary tale reported of a tanker from the Chinese mainland which got into difficulties off a rural coastline. It was said that the tanker crew spoke Mandarin and the local Chinese restaurant worker, found by the police or coast guards, spoke Cantonese and the subsequent oil spill was extensive.

Codes also usually state 'or accept delegated assignments without con-sent'. This also covers those instances when, for example, the original interpreter rings a suitably qualified colleague from a hospital accident and emergency department where she or he has taken their *own* child following a domestic accident, thereby preventing them from attending the agreed interpreting assignment. The second interpreter is asked if she or he can deal with the planned assignment and is given the bare details and the contact number of the principal. The second interpreter then immediately contacts the principal, explains the situation and, if available for the assignment, supplies his or her own qualifications and, where these exist, professional registration number. Again, the onus is on the principal to make the decision and a new letter of agreement on terms has to be requested in the new name.

All the above also applies to those times when an interpreter is offered a four-week contract to interpret in, for example, a long court case but has already accepted a one-hour assignment to assist a lawyer during those dates. The principle that all assignments should be honoured stands, but there are usually ways around circumstances such as these. People do understand the situation if it is explained to them honestly and fairly. A substitute of equal competence might well be available through the proper channels. The lawyer might well be able to change the time or date of the appointment. In the last resort, however, the previously accepted short, one-hour assignment should be honoured.

Interpreters and translators shall not:

(e) **use any information gained during the course of their work for the benefit of themselves or anyone else**
(f) **accept any reward arising from an assignment other than the agreed fees and expenses**

The first proscription is, one hopes, particularly self-evident. Although public service interpreters are unlikely to have the opportunity to be tempted to become involved in insider dealing in the realms of high finance, they do come across other types of information that could be abused. This might include such information as planning applications for buildings and businesses.

Declining presents and favours is particularly crucial when working in the public services and sometimes requires considerable finesse and firmness. There are particular cultures where the giving of presents and favours is not only acceptable but is expected. This may include not being allowed to pay for meals in restaurants where the owner, or a member of his family, has been assisted by the interpreter in the course of professional duty. In other cultures, such as the UK, this is not only unacceptable but also frowned upon; a small box of chocolates, a thank you note or a bunch of flowers is the recognised limit for expressing appreciation. Refusal can appear discourteous and ungracious to someone from another culture. Such culture clashes can be addressed, on a wider scale, through community leaders of the language groups who let it be known that this is the correct approach. In countries where matters are conducted differently, there should perhaps be some sort of agreement reached so that there is never a perception that the quality of service given is dependent upon the quality of gifts or favours received by the interpreter.

Any attempt at bribery or corruption, or even the suspicion of it, has to be reported immediately to the authorities. There are those who may wish the interpreter to misinterpret, for example, witnesses in criminal proceedings. This may be rare but it is well not to be naïve and then be compromised and even frightened by not knowing how to respond, how to anticipate such problems or how to avoid situations where it might happen.

(g) Interpreters and translators shall seek to increase their professional skills and knowledge

The injunction to continue developing as a professional applies to professionals everywhere. Languages, language usage and public service procedures and structures change constantly and move on. Interpreters are only as good as their grasp of current language usage and situations. Continuing professional and personal development is discussed in Chapter 4 under the general topic of training.

(h) safeguard professional standards and offer assistance to other interpreters and translators whenever reasonable, practical and appropriate

This aim is also held in common with other professions and is addressed in three broad areas. Interpreters and translators have a responsibility to the profession as a whole: to its standards, its body of knowledge, its reputation and its members. Standards need to be and are safeguarded by, for example, creating national benchmarks of skills and by trained interpreters acting as examiners and promoting best practice in ways which go beyond their individual interests.

Some professional codes include the necessity to behave in a manner befitting a professional in all aspects of life. This is perhaps particularly

relevant where the interpreter is a member of a small language community, where a good personal reputation contributes to the necessary
trust. This can sometimes have problematic aspects, where what is considered to be respectable behaviour in one culture is not in another.
A female interpreter may, for example, wear a sleeveless summer blouse
or a male interpreter may date someone outside the language community, which are considered perfectly proper in one culture but not in
the other. Interpreters are bicultural and they may have to judge their
behaviour quite finely. On the other hand, getting drunk in public on a
regular basis is likely to be unacceptable in many cultures. One of the
criteria for belonging to a professional register is the absence of relevant
criminal convictions.

In the public services it is self-evident that anyone should offer assistance to colleagues, for example, by sharing terminology. As the profession evolves, this is increasingly becoming formalised through mentoring
and supervision strategies, whereby more experienced practitioners can
help and support those new to the profession.

Interpreters and translators have a primary responsibility to safeguard
their own profession's standards in the interests of both the public services and the other-language speakers. They can find this uncomfortable
if, for example, they come across a misinterpretation or inaccurate
translation that happened earlier in a particular matter and has an effect
upon outcomes, because that should be reported to the public service
involved whether or not they themselves were responsible. It can be
hard to do, but it can be done discreetly through accepted protocols. It
may be that an otherwise reliable linguist has made a genuine mistake
and can appreciate a colleague's vigilance. At the other extreme, there
may be negligence or incompetence of an order that has to be dealt with
robustly, if it is not to continue in future assignments.

The development of such a professional approach has sometimes been
problematic. Public service professionals have at times been shocked and
embarrassed, for example, by interpreters and translators complaining
publicly, and in an inappropriate manner, about other interpreters and
translators. Such unacceptable behaviour could give rise to the suspicion
that the complainant is seeking to gain unfair financial advantage. This
does not mean that substandard practice should not be recognised
and dealt with, provided that the evidence for it can be substantiated,
but rather that it should be done through formal established strategies
that are effective and discreet. The disciplinary procedures, that will be
described in Chapter 5, encompass what is needed for those who belong
to a professional register. If, however, immediate action is needed or the

person concerned is not a member of a language professional body, then careful consideration should be given to how to bring the matter quickly and appropriately to the attention of the public service personnel involved, who may wish to terminate the agreement with the interpreter or translator concerned pending proper investigation of the complaint.

(i)   Interpreters and translators shall observe confidentiality

Interpreters and translators must treat as confidential any information that may come to them in the course of their work. This may also include the fact that they have undertaken a particular assignment. This does not preclude making use of such experiences on an anonymous and strictly confidential basis, within the recognised structures of professional support and training where colleagues are bound to observe the same codes. This addendum allows interpreters and translators to seek appropriate support and help when they need it.

Confidentiality not only has to be observed, it has to be seen to be observed. Only then can other-language speakers and the public services extend trust to interpreters and translators in the same way that everyone should be able to know that doctors do not discuss a patient's ailments with anyone else other than professional colleagues.

There are very rare occasions when confidentiality can be broken and then only under established requirements. In the UK, for example, there is a legal requirement that any one who suspects child abuse should report it to the proper authorities immediately.

Enquiries from third parties as to what took place during an assignment may arise from no more than simple human curiosity. Those who remember the days when children were used as interpreters know that, on their return home, their mothers, aunts and cousins all wanted to know what had happened at the solicitor's offices or doctor's surgery and it was a brave child who pretended not to remember. Even for adults it is tempting to gossip or to indicate that one is privy to information that others would like to know. Knowledge is power and therefore potentially enjoyable, but also dangerous.

There may be people skilled in persuasion, who attempt to pressure interpreters and translators into breaking confidentiality. Other parties in criminal cases, relatives in domestic disputes or neighbours in social matters may all have an interest in pumping the interpreter for information. If care is taken to make it generally known that this is not acceptable and why, they may not even try. If they do try, they should be deflected from doing so. The interpreter should have support in this from their professional body, the relevant public service and, indeed, from the other-language speaking community. In particular, assignments should never ever be discussed with members of the press, although most reputable reporters are aware of the interpreters' code and will not make such an approach.

(j)   **interpret and translate truly and faithfully, to the best of one's ability, without anything being added or omitted; summarising only when requested and with the knowledge and consent of all parties**

(k)   **observe, and be seen to observe, impartiality**

These are the code items still under debate by some who would have the 'interpreter' act in other and additional capacities and be partial. This approach is often but not always accompanied by a claim that the standard of language skills realistically required as a minimum to be able to 'interpret and translate truly and faithfully without anything being added or omitted', is elitist and unnecessary, and that lower level skills are acceptable and adequate to the task.

The proponents of this approach would wish the 'interpreters' to act as advocates for what they see as one 'side' or another. As in the examples described below, this might include: selecting and formulating information to be exchanged in ways which they personally think might suit the purpose better, tidying up an other-language speaker's utterances so that they sound more coherent, adding information to messages explaining medical terms and procedures, adding advice and opinions such as how to answer questions and screening out information such as that deemed by the interpreter to be irrelevant or culturally inappropriate.

This mainly happens where the public service personnel have not been trained to work with interpreters or across cultures and where the interpreter does not trust them to do so effectively and is not equipped with the strategies to help them do so. While this could be seen as a valid approach in such circumstances, it carries significant risks that are worth discussing.

A primary point is the accuracy of the information which is transferred by the interpreter. The principal participants in an exchange, that is the other-language speaker and the public service employee, need to know precisely what the other is saying. If, for instance, the other-language speaker is expressing himself or herself in an incoherent, rambling fashion then the doctor, police officer or social worker needs to know because it can indicate much about the other-language speaker's state of mind or educational background. If the interpreter decides to 'tidy up' other-language speaker utterances into formal, calm, orderly ways of expressing information, all that essential information can be lost. If the utterances of, say, a doctor attempting to elicit information through a tentative questioning process on sensitive matters are not appropriately rendered, then the communication fails (cf. for example, Cambridge: 1999). For example, 'do you like to have a couple of glasses of wine to relax you when you are worried?' does not necessarily mean 'do you drink a lot?'

Furthermore, the interpreter cannot always know what is relevant to the public service, or *vice versa*, and there could be damaging outcomes if anything is omitted. Public service personnel try to say precisely what they mean and, if there is any ambiguity, the interpreter should clarify exactly what is meant. When a mother brings into hospital a small son who has fallen off a swing and banged his head, one of the questions the mother will be asked is, 'has he been sick, or said he felt sick?' In the UK, unlike the US, in this context, 'to be sick' means 'to vomit', 'feeling sick' means 'nauseous'. Both are symptoms of potential brain damage. To transfer the meaning of 'sick' as 'ill' or only to ask one part of the question could elicit a dangerously misleading answer.

Vital clues as to medical symptoms may be encoded in throwaway comments. For example: 'This cough is exhausting, my ribs are hurting. I am having a terrible time at school and then I feel dreadful when I throw up'. It is the last fact that is symptomatic of whooping cough.

Witnesses to crimes may not themselves realise the significance of a detail. For example: 'There was a big bang. I saw this car swerving onto the pavement and he nearly hit a lady with a pram . . . We all shouted, including the guy on the motor bike'. Who was the guy on the motor-bike and was he involved in the crash? Is he a potential useful witness? Skilled police officers are trained in how people remember things and will be careful about how facts are elicited, so that they can be relied upon in court.

Family members often tuck away important feelings relevant to the matter in hand, but which they are reluctant to express overtly, into snatches of phrases. The skilled social worker can gently bring these out into the open in ways that respect sensitivities and can lead to practical and emotional solutions. For example: 'We are all anxious to look after granny because it is our duty. She is no trouble really. She eats quite well and doesn't trouble us much in the night. We do have a washing machine to do her sheets every day and keep the doors locked because she got out once and a neighbour found her in the street in her nightie.

The kids are very fond of her but they don't bring their friends home much anymore.' Incontinence and potential dementia require help but all of that utterance has to be transferred accurately into the target language, so that the social worker can work with the family towards realistic and practical solutions.

Nor should anything be omitted because it is distasteful. Swearing is often no more than a sign of anger or frustration and that needs to be known (Cambridge 2005). Descriptions of rape and sexual abuse in criminal cases have to be precise and explicit. Paraphrasing such descriptions into 'he behaved disrespectfully' on the grounds that 'ladies in my culture do not use such words' does not help anyone. This is well illustrated in a video made by Vancouver Community College Open Learning Agency in 2000, entitled *Points of Departure – Ethical Challenges for Court and Community Interpreters*. Medical terms, in both formal and informal registers, have to be known and used appropriately. Waving distantly towards 'down there' does not aid a useful diagnosis. There are usually a couple of dozen informal words for 'penis' and 'vulva' in any language.

Interpreters are responsible for the communication process and they can intervene for three reasons, described in the general guidelines to good practice below, to keep that intact. There are risks involved if they take on additional roles and, for example, add their own advice or personal opinions to the other-language speaker or the public service. If interpreters add their own advice or opinion, they are likely to get things wrong or at best be inadequate to the task for which they are neither qualified nor insured. Furthermore, should matters go awry, it would be subsequently very difficult to sort out who had said what to whom and on what basis, whether or not litigation were involved. The other-language speaker is the person who knows best where their pain is, what they saw, what they feel and what they wish to happen in a situation. Public services are used to dealing with clients who are frightened or anxious, who have education or mental health difficulties or who do not know how the system works, and should be allowed to do so. The lawyer, doctor, nurse, social worker or teacher is the best person to know their professional business and therefore the best person to inform the other-language speaker directly and to answer any questions.

The interpreter should not become an active third party to the information exchange. In most public service interactions, it is important that there is a direct relationship between the public service personnel and the member of the public concerned. The doctor/patient and lawyer/client relationship, for example, is an integral part of the professional process and the interpreter should promote this relationship rather than impede it. This is separate from the relationship of trust which both parties should have with the interpreter.

Where the interpreter does take on additional responsibilities on behalf of both the public service personnel and the other-language speaker, such as explaining legal procedures or cultural customs, it discourages them from assuming those responsibilities. If competent interpreting and adequate information and opportunity are provided, it is likely that other-language speakers are capable of explaining themselves, asking questions and comprehending what is happening.

It is often said by proponents of the advocacy approach that public service personnel, particularly doctors and judges, are un-trainable in matters relating to working with language professionals and across cultures. This has proved to be without foundation where the necessary training, support and structures have been put in place (cf. Chapter 7). The requirement to treat everyone equally, irrespective of language and culture, is, in many countries such as the UK, part of the code of conduct of every profession and is also required by statute (*Race Relations Act 1976*). Where this is in place, professional disciplinary and, if necessary, legal procedures can be invoked to ensure observance by the public services. The responsibility for the skills to work with interpreters and across cultures lies firmly with the public service discipline concerned.

Finally, accurate interpreting demands high levels of concentration. If the interpreters are also doing other things at the same time, and making themselves morally responsible for what others are saying and doing, the level of accuracy is likely to diminish.

Therefore, for the reasons listed above, the conclusion is being drawn that the preferred and most reliable approach in cases where there is no shared language, is to have a qualified, impartial interpreter working with public service personnel who are trained and equipped to deliver their service across languages and cultures.

The concept of public service personnel who have been trained and assessed in both linguistic and professional skills to deliver their expertise through two languages (as 'bilingual practitioners'), and therefore do not need the assistance of an interpreter, is discussed in Chapter 6.

The general guidelines to interpreting good practice

These have evolved in the light of experience to support the implementation of the codes. Sometimes practical situations get in the way of the guidelines being followed in detail, as already indicated in our discussion of key points in a Code of Conduct.

The good practice requirements for accepting an assignment have been described earlier in this chapter. Once the assignment has been accepted, the interpreter arrives at the designated venue ahead of time to meet the public service contact person, to present their identification badge with their photograph and to make themselves ready. They take this opportunity to find out whether there have been any changes since the arrangements were made, such as whether other procedures have taken place or whether the original estimated time allowed for the assignment has altered.

At the outset of the interview, formal introductions are made. Through the interpreter, the public service practitioner introduces him- or herself to the other-language speaker, saying their name clearly and describing their role and, if necessary, their rank and qualifications. The other-language speaker cannot necessarily read the significance of uniforms. The public service practitioner then ensures that they know and can pronounce the other-language speaker's name correctly and greet them accordingly.

Then the interpreter is introduced last to signify that they are not the principals in the exchange. The interpreter will then explain, in both languages but first to the other-language speaker: how they wish to be addressed, that they will interpret everything that is said without adding anything or leaving anything out, that they will be impartial and that they will observe absolute confidentiality and will only interrupt if they feel that the communication is slipping.

Interpreters may then say that they propose that everyone uses direct speech or, because not many people understand what direct speech is, may gently nudge their clients into it after the start of the conversation, by saying something like: 'We will find it easier if you talk to each other directly, instead of to me. Just say, "I am glad to meet you", rather than "Tell her I am glad to meet her" and I will interpret.' If the participants persist in addressing the interpreter, rather than each other, it is often useful for the interpreter simply to look down at their notepad to avoid eye contact, so that the principal participants have to look at each other.

The introductory stage is also used to re-check the language match between the interpreter and the other-language speaker in particular. If mutual comprehension cannot be established, consideration should be given to contacting a more appropriate interpreter.

As indicated above, two-way consecutive interpreting, i.e. into and out of each language by conversational turn, is the most frequently used technique in most public service interactions. And whispered interpreting is used where occasion demands it. The most usual examples of this technique are particular stages during court hearings when the other-language speaker is not part of the exchange, for example, during the judge's summing up or where a long utterance should not be interrupted, for example, when strong emotions are being expressed. In such cases, the interpreter chooses not to interrupt the flow of the conversation; they may interpret simultaneously into either language. Guidelines recommend that the interpreter can intervene to preserve the communication for four specific reasons:

1. To ask for accommodation to the interpreting process, for example, when someone is speaking inaudibly or too quickly.
2. To ask for clarification of an utterance that is ambiguous, unclear or contains a term that is not understood by the interpreter. This may be a technical term or slang.
3. To alert the participants that someone may not have understood what has been said, although the interpreting was correct. Interpreters have a good feel for comprehension and can sense when this is happening. The causes may be various but they can, for example, include either party using formal registers or technical terms that are not comprehensible to the other in either language.
4. To alert the participants that a relevant cultural inference may have been missed. This refers to an item of information that is not in the cultural frame of reference of one or more of the participants. An example could be the significance of religious festivals and why it was important that a family member should be home for Christmas, Divali and so on.

Having alerted the participants to the last two points, the interpreter does not give their *own* explanations but rather passes the matter back to the principals, with perhaps the suggestion that 'you may wish to ask your client about the significance of Divali', and then interpret their explanations. It is essential that the interventions are made in both languages, following the normal interpreter convention that nothing is said in one language during an assignment unless the content is also shared with the other participant.

Interpreters can be asked to comment on relevant linguistic matters, and will do so in both languages. There are times, usually in court hearings, where more is needed by way of linguistic or cultural explanation. Then the interpreter will, if qualified to do so, step out of their interpreter role and become an expert witness. Each statement made by an expert witness has to be factually accurate or, where not known to be so, suitable *caveats* are given. If the interpreter does not feel qualified to comment on the matter germane to the case, then another person must be called who is.

Normally, the interpreted exchange settles down to its own rhythm and, if all goes well, the principals feel they are communicating with each other. The interpreter will take notes, particularly of names and numbers, in the normal way of note-taking by interpreters trained in consecutive work (see Gillies 2005). These, although usually incomprehensible to anyone but the interpreter, are handed in to be destroyed at the end of the assignment. It is a matter of being seen to observe confidentiality. The interpreter may, however, note any new terminology or procedures, which do not impact on confidentiality, for their own future use.

There may have to be reminders over and above the original explanation about the interpreter's role during the subsequent exchange when, for example, a defendant is on the brink of saying 'I'm guilty but don't tell them' or a social worker asks 'Is she telling the truth?' It has also happened that attempts are made to manipulate the interpreter and these have to be guarded against, for example, 'You too are a devout Christian/Muslim/Hindu, so tell them that I could not possibly have done this' or 'This patient is a pain in the neck. Can you get her to shut up?' To which the interpreter may reply, 'I stated at the outset that I would interpret everything that was said. Shall I interpret that?' On the other hand, observing impartiality does not necessarily preclude gently holding the hand of someone recently bereaved or appropriately comforting a child.

Before the conclusion of the assignment, the next practical steps to be undertaken are interpreted, including whether the interpreter is to be called again; availabilities are then checked. The necessary paperwork is completed in connection with the interpreter's fees and, if required, logbooks are signed.

Afterwards, the interpreter and the public service practitioner may reflect together on the linguistic content of the assignment and consider what they could learn from their performances to improve in the future. The service content is not the interpreter's responsibility and it is not their role to discuss the quality of, say, the medical care provided, which is a matter for the medical profession.

At home, the interpreter will file any non-confidential information which it may be useful to retrieve quickly in the future such as information leaflets on procedures, drugs, terminology or useful practical tips.

Guidelines to Good Practice for Specific Purposes

Guidelines of this kind support the implementation of codes of practice and of the general guidelines to good practice for specific activities. Specific Guidelines are usually developed and piloted, in collaboration with the relevant public service whose personnel will observe parallel and complementary guidelines. An example is the following extract from the National Agreement on arrangements for the use of interpreters, translators and language professionals in investigations and proceedings within the Criminal Justice System (England and Wales) as revised in 2007, reproduced here:

8. Ensuring interpreter safety

8.1 Those responsible for requesting the attendance of interpreters should take responsibility for ensuring their safety.

8.2 Police officers should ensure that the interpreter can verify any request to attend a place that is not a public building – for example by providing them with a number at the police station to call back and confirm their assignment. Officers making the request should also carry out a risk assessment in relation to the interpreter's attendance. They should consider whether, for example, the interpreter should be met at a suitable place such as a police station or train station before proceeding to the property where the assignment is to take place in the company of police. They will also want to ensure the interpreter is properly briefed on the situation and that their safety is considered whilst they carry out the assignment.

8.3 An interpreter should never be left in a room/cell with the person he/she is interpreting for without a member of staff in attendance. Similarly, interpreters should never leave police stations at the same time or through the same entrances and exits as interviewees with whom they have worked.

The development of guidelines for specific purposes promotes the necessary forward planning in organising interpreting services, for example, in the planning required for major emergencies, when the interdisciplinary team has to be capable of arriving ready to operate together at the highest level straight away. The time spent rehearsing for such events by many of the other public services rarely includes interpreters, even though other-language speakers are very often involved.

That exercise gives rise to the need for answers to the following questions. How can sufficient numbers of interpreters, in the languages needed, be contacted in an emergency on a 24/7 basis? If there is a professional register for interpreters that can be accessed, which interpreters would be needed, what should be their particular qualifications and what in-service training should they have had? Should they have been asked in advance whether this is something they are prepared to do and would age and physical or psychological fitness be considerations? How will the interpreters get to the site and gain access? What should they bring with them – should they have been issued with, to carry in their trusty bag of kit and in addition to their identification badges, fluorescent tabards with, on the front and back, **INTERPRETER: SPANISH/ESPAGNOL AND ENGLISH** or whatever their working languages are? Are pre-designed letters of agreement in place and is insurance an issue?

Upon arrival, who should the interpreters report to immediately and what are their subsequent communication lines? How will their tasks be allocated, what will their responsibilities and accountability be, and what record-keeping would be expected? What general and personal safety and security protocols would have to be observed? Given that there are limits to stamina, where can food and drink be obtained and how long should their shifts be if the situation lasts longer than two or three hours? What arrangements have been planned to communicate with relatives of the injured and others making enquiries and how would the enquirers' and the interpreters' languages be matched? How will the interpreters leave the incident safely and reach their home destinations? What support would be given to interpreters during and after the incident?

It is this example, of what one hopes is a rare assignment, that illustrates well the benefit of in-service training and preparation, and also of education in its widest sense. Public service interpreters usually work alone. A true understanding of their role and of their codes and guidelines stands them in good stead, and benefits others, in whatever situation they find themselves in.

Suggested activities

- look up the codes of conduct of the national professional language body, if you have one in your country
- look up, and compare, the codes of conduct relating to other professions, such as medicine, nursing and law

- ask a member of another professional discipline about their guidelines to good practice for particular procedures
- talk to a Health & Safety Officer about their responsibilities

Suggested further reading

Alcaraz, E. and Hughes, B. (2002) *Legal Translation Explained*. Manchester: St Jerome.

Bell, R. (1991) *Translation and Translating: Theory and Practice*. London: Longman.

Bolden, G. B. (2000) 'Toward Understanding Practices of Medical Interpreting: Interpreters' Involvement in History Taking', *Discourse Studies* 2(4): 387–419.

Davidson, B. (2001) 'Questions in cross-linguistic medical encounters: the role of the hospital interpreter', *Anthropological Quarterly* 74(4): 170–8.

Englund Dimitrova, B. (1997) 'Degree of interpreter responsibility in the interaction process in community interpreting', in A. Carr, R. Roberts, A. Dufour and D. Steyn (eds) *The Critical Link 1. Interpreters in the Community*. Amsterdam: John Benjamins: 147–63.

Fraser, J. (1999) 'The Discourse of Official Texts and How it Can Impede Public Service Translators', *Journal of Multilingual and Multicultural Development* 20(3): 194–208.

Hale, Sandra (2007) *Community Interpreting* Basingstoke/New York: Palgrave Macmillan.

Montalt, V. and González Davies, M. (2007) *Medical Translation Step By Step*. Manchester: St Jerome.

Jacobs, B., Kroll, L., Green, J. and David, J. (1995) 'The hazards of using a child as an interpreter', *Journal of the Royal Society of Medicine* 88 August 474–5.

Pöchhacker, F. (2000) 'The Community Interpreter's task: self-perception and provider views', in Roberts R., Carr S., Abraham D. and Dufour A. *The Critical Link 2: Interpreters in the Community*. Amsterdam: John Benjamins 49–65.

Pöchhacker, F. and Kadric, M. (1999) 'The Hospital Cleaner as Healthcare Interpreter: A Case Study', *The Translator* 5(2): 161–78.

Wadensjö, C. (1993) 'The double role of a dialogue interpreter', *Perspectives. Studies in Translatology* 1: 105–21 [reprinted in F. Pöchhacker and M. Shlesinger (eds) (2002) *The Interpreting Studies Reader*. London: Routledge].

Websites

www.najit.org (The National Association of Judiciary Interpreters and Translators (USA))

www.naati.com.au (The National Accreditation Authority for Translators and Interpreters Ltd (Australia))

www.nrpublic service interpreter.org.uk (The National Register of Public Service Interpreters Ltd (UK))

http://www.vera.org/publications/publications.asp (VERA Institute of Justice)

4
Training and Assessment of Public Service Interpreters

Conference interpreting is perhaps the best-known branch of interpreting. Training normally includes a first degree in languages, followed by a period of intensive postgraduate specialised training. Although the standards required are the same, this recognised training route is not yet often available to public service interpreters. Nevertheless, the selection, training and assessment of public service interpreters has much in common with other career paths followed by those graduating from language degrees. In many countries, however, that process is less well established, less well recognised and less well paid than other areas of work.

The main cause for this difference in training opportunities lies in the lack of commitment on the part of the authorities to insist on the level of competence needed in the public service context and to provide the necessary resources and structures to reach it. As discussed in Chapter 1, the increasing demand for public service interpreters and translators has been recognised for over 20 years. With a few notable exceptions, such as Australia and Sweden, few countries have yet dealt robustly with that challenge. There are few postgraduate courses in public service interpreting and, indeed, few full-time courses at undergraduate level.

Nonetheless, considerable progress has been made based upon the art of the possible, driven by a pressing need and without much by way of tradition specific to the field. This clean slate has led to a range of imaginative and innovative approaches to training, often carried out on a shoestring, by multidisciplinary teams of enthusiastic and committed individuals. These have included the UNISA (University of South Africa, http://www.unisa.ac.za) BA in court interpreting, where students may not be able to attend classes because, in many areas, public transport is minimal and travel can be dangerous. There may be no access to computers to aid distance learning, even where there are electricity supplies.

In Canada, the Vancouver Community College staff has devised distance learning materials to cope with their climate and distances and the communities in or near the Arctic circle. In Australia training has for some time been matched to climatic and geographical conditions of a different sort by combining distance learning with short face-to-face courses. Climate, distance and electricity supplies may not affect European countries but there are other challenges often held in common. These include the scarcity of qualified graduate language tutors in the range of languages required, uneven levels of existing language skills and a lack of appropriate teaching materials.

The lodestar has been the standards and type of skills needed for the tasks to be done in the workplace. These have been elicited through observation and by taking soundings from those already working in the field. These analyses have largely been unrecorded because there was not the time or energy to do so. However, they accord with the broad international consensus of what is required to produce accurate and reliable interpreting and translation. They have been derived from professional expertise and common sense, combined with collaborative insights from language communities and public service professionals.

The standards are rigorous and necessary and are proving themselves in the field. They do, of course, have to be constantly defended against authorities who do not wish to pay for a proper standard of skills and the rather confusing picture of different levels of qualification – often not made explicit – from a range of educational establishments. Such 'qualifications' may in some cases simply be certificates of attendance, rather than an attestation of fully assessed skills at an appropriate level.

How one reaches the standards can be flexible. Training is geared not just to passing qualifying examinations, but beyond that to preparing for good professional practice and development. Gradually, worthwhile training opportunities are growing as the adequately trained and qualified interpreters earn respect from the front line public service professionals who, in turn, are putting pressure on their managers. Inadequacies that once went unnoticed are being challenged, particularly in the legal context.

This is happening cumulatively through a range of activities. For example, a police officer who had acted as an interlocutor for examination role plays, described his experience as follows:

> I had no idea what good interpreting meant at the start of the day. Then this candidate came in whom I knew. I have always thought him very good because he wears a suit and tie and speaks very fast

in both languages. When he had done his test, the examiner, who spoke both languages, was re-checking carefully what had been said with both us interlocutors and it became clear to me that neither the facts or the nuance had been interpreted accurately. Then this other guy came in and I thought he wouldn't be up to much because he was a bit diffident and informally dressed. He spoke quite slowly but it turned out his interpreting was accurate. It was scary to think of the risks we have been running in our service because, until now, we have just trusted anyone who came in and said they could speak a foreign language and we have no means of knowing, do we? I am going back to my colleagues straight away and we will talk to our boss about making sure we get properly qualified interpreters in future.

Previously untapped language potential among people who may or may not have had an opportunity to undergo tertiary education is proving to be significant. A university language tutor who came to assist with training was impressed by the factory worker who thought nothing of being able to listen to a speech in one language, make notes in a second language and give it back in a third language. So the target levels and types of skills are identified, the existing language potential is recognised and the work is being done to bridge the gap.

Collaboration between branches of the language profession

One of the reasons why today's language students will recognise common principles is that in many countries, certainly in the UK, conference interpreters and senior linguists from other fields have made a valuable contribution to the process of developing training and assessments. As experienced professionals, they were able to apply their expertise to contribute to problem-solving in an unfamiliar area of work.

On one occasion, members of AIIC (International Association of Conference Interpreters, see http://www.aiic.net/) became used to half their class decamping, in the middle of a lesson on interpreting theory, to help in the police station across the road. Indeed, they joined their students and were fascinated by the use of registers and terminology they did not usually come across and then incorporated those into their classes. They contributed bravely to what is known as 'Red Face Day', which is always a testing part of training, when students undertake classroom role plays involving such matters as rape, sexual abuse and indecent exposure. These days are designed to help students overcome their embarrassment and reluctances in the privacy of the classroom so that, faced with the inevitable reality of having to interpret in such situations, they can put aside their own feelings and concentrate on interpreting every nuance accurately, impartially and without hesitation. On the other hand, when a student was challenged for being late for class, she wearily replied that she had been up all night 'having a baby', an experience not familiar to conference interpreters in that sense. Translators from other fields have also helped in devising strategies for dealing with the imperfections in the source text to render a meaning in the target language that is comprehensible to its intended readership.

Understanding negative pressures

Anyone who is interested in being involved in training public service interpreters needs to know what they might be up against. An essential part of being involved in a new development process includes gaining a realistic understanding of potential obstacles to progress in order to overcome them. In the area of training and assessment there is a clear negative cycle to be broken. Inadequate training and assessment leads to inadequately qualified 'interpreters' who are likely to be inappropriately used, poorly paid, vulnerable, without prospects and a risk to others. This leads to lack of recognition of skills, which leads to lack of training and so on. Robust responses, and patience, are needed to pursue adequate standards.

Being aware of the agendas of organisations and individuals allows one to evaluate them objectively and to work with them or around them. In summary, there are five main obstacles to establishing proper training and assessments.

Translators and interpreters, as yet, normally have no protection of title. Nor is there yet an established system whereby training courses, such as in the legal and medical professions, are accredited as a safeguard to professional standards. Despite efforts to the contrary, there are pressures within further and higher education motivated by short-term economic considerations rather than primarily by academic or professional ones, even though these might bring better long-term economic success. It is therefore possible to fill places and gather student fees by offering courses to train interpreters in ten hours or three days and then to offer a certificate at, or below, school leaving level. It is indicative that when someone who was responsible for such an initiative was challenged, she reportedly said that it was 'only' for interpreting in the health service.

The mainstream academic framework is only now beginning to encompass the subject of public service interpreting. This may have been because of a perceived lack of status and standards involved in the public service field and the range of languages involved, which are outside those normally dealt with by academia. More to the point, much traditional university language teaching is not designed for the public service context so that few would have the specialist expertise to teach in that area. In many language degrees the curriculum is based on the history, literature and institutions of the target-language country or countries, including also the contemporary standard variety of the target language. Other university courses teach conference interpreting, or interpreting and translation for use in commercial or international settings. All such courses have their role to play but there is a need for an alternative approach, and additional specialist teaching skills, for the public service field.

Potential public service interpreters are mainly mature people who require an income to meet their family commitments. They are likely to have little by way of the financial backing to pay university fees, and the subject is not yet sufficiently established to make them eligible for university grants in those countries where these exist. Nor are they in a position to risk investing time and energy in a training that may bring them low and unpredictable incomes. The immediate challenge, until better times prevail, is therefore to provide a worthwhile training that is accessible, affordable and allows students to meet their other commitments.

From the public service point of view, there is an increasing immediate demand for public service interpreters. Those involved in the decision-making for implementing the arrangements are unlikely to have a sound understanding of the type and standard of graduate language skills needed, and may indeed prefer not to know because of the short-term costs: employing interpreters with degree-level qualifications means higher fees. Most administrators are constrained by short-term budgets, and targets may favour cosmetic quick fixes. The challenge in this regard is to persuade public services of the need for an incremental planned route to acceptable standards and for responsible ways of dealing with interim shortcomings.

There are many people who have been working as interpreters for years, as best they could without meaningful training or assessment. They may be understandably reluctant to undergo either for fear of losing face and/or their meagre income; they often argue strenuously against the need to have their skills challenged or improved. There have been examples of almost a third of such untrained interpreters failing to pass a relatively simple test to see whether they were suitable for interpreter training. In the absence of appropriate training, however, the remainder were denied the opportunity to develop, despite showing great potential. Professional examinations are also seen by some as elit-ist and pro-establishment.

Given such obstacles, it is remarkable that so many students have suc-cessfully attended demanding part-time courses in addition to working for a living or looking after a family. Such courses are often made possi-ble by language teachers and public service personnel making contribu-tions, often in their free time and beyond the call of duty.

Perceptions are gradually changing: qualified interpreters are proving their worth and their standards are being accepted. They are attracting reasonable fees and being treated with more professional respect in some countries. Where this happens, more and more suitably qualified students are applying for training and assessment. As a consequence, more training is made available leading to responsible standards, and the negative cycle is reversed.

Likely language starting points

As mentioned at the beginning of this chapter, potential public service interpreters are likely to lack a formal first degree in languages normally held by those planning to become conference interpreters. There is unlikely to exist, therefore, a predictable and consistent set of existing skills as a foundation for further training. However, while the starting points may be different and uneven, they may be equally valuable. It is a matter of recognising objectively what skills exist, enhancing them in ways that are accessible and the rest follows on.

There is a range of variables affecting existing language starting points, depending upon the circumstances and life experience of the individual. There are different types and degrees of bilingualism (see, for instance, Romaine 1995) with few individuals being equally proficient in all areas in both (or more) languages. For example, it is unlikely that there will be a balance between the levels of proficiency, competencies (reading, writ-ing, listening, speaking) and the domains of use. One language, not nec-essarily the mother tongue, is likely to be dominant.

Children of other-language speaking parents who have been schooled through the medium of the majority language, are more likely to use their parents' language in the domestic context and the majority lan-guage for higher education, work, leisure pursuits with their peers and general reading. This means that they could, for example, possess the terminology necessary to organise a mortgage in their second language but not in their first language. Equally, they might be able to describe a favourite dish of their mother's only in their domestic language. Literacy skills may be undeveloped in their heritage language despite parents' efforts to send children to supplementary classes after school. The fact that bilinguals 'rarely have identical knowledge in other languages' has been given as a reason why 'many bilinguals are not effective at inter- pretation and translation' (Baker 2000: 82). In other words, training is required, particularly in order to extend certain areas of vocabulary.

People who settle in a country when they are older tend to have a flu- ent command of their first language and acquire a command of the sec- ond language. How good the command of the first language, particularly the literacy levels, can depend upon the opportunities available for edu- cation in their country of origin rather than the ability of the individual. Education is often the first casualty of war, natural disasters or economic hardships. The level of command of the second language (L2) can depend upon the availability of learning opportunities. Individuals can be caught in a vicious circle, whereby their inadequate command of the majority language results in their having to take employment which demands long hours of physically demanding work for low pay, leaving little time and energy for learning or improving a second language.

A first language can become dormant due to lack of constant and comprehensive use, and can be experienced as a subtle bereavement. Students speak with both wonder and sadness at the imperceptible trickling away of their abilities to express the nuances of their feelings and thoughts in a once familiar tongue. One day they find they cannot write to relatives, as surely as they once did, letters of condolence or exchange ideas about literature and politics or answer their children's questions about the grammar and vocabulary of the language that is part of their heritage.

Ignoring or minimising the implications of the range and type of existing starting skills in relation to the target skills that need to be achieved handicaps future progress. Those skills may contain a wider and deeper linguistic and cultural potential, of the sort needed in the public service field, than can be gained through formal academic study. Nonetheless, a solid written and spoken command of both languages is needed before *interpreter* training can begin.

Each potential student's skills may differ according to their individual life experiences, education and language acquisition. It has often been found useful therefore to conduct preliminary assessments for potential interpreter students and to provide them with incremental steps to the levels needed to begin interpreter training. Such incremental steps may take the form of an access course or remedial teaching on individual aspects, for example, to raise the level of literacy in one language. It also has to be accepted that some individuals may have the potential to further develop their language skills but not to acquire interpreting skills.

Assessment

Formal assessments should take place at the following points of career development. These should, wherever possible, be calibrated against independent national occupational standards e.g. *National Occupational Standards for Interpreters* in the UK (www.CILT.org.uk/standards).

- at the end of access courses, designed to build a firm foundation for further training
- at initial professional level (honours first degree level/equivalent)
- at postgraduate professional level
- and for Continuing Professional Development (CPD) throughout a career.

In all public service professions, an objective prior assessment of skills, before being allowed to practise unsupervised, is a prerequisite in an arena where grave responsibilities are undertaken and potential risks are significant. In summary, the skills required by a public service interpreter include:

- knowledge of the relevant public service, its structure, procedures, processes and personnel
- written and spoken fluency in both the relevant languages, including the commonly used range of relevant registers and terminology
- the ability to transfer meaning accurately between languages, both ways, including:
  - two-way consecutive interpreting
  - whispered simultaneous interpreting (including the ability to go in both directions)
  - sight translation
  - translation of short written texts
- understanding of the code of ethics and of strategies to implement it
- strategies for professional and personal continuous development.

General principles governing assessments

No assessment ever covers all aspects of practice. A combination of assessment methods, such as a formal examination plus on-the-job assessments is more likely to provide a truer picture.

To be useful, assessments should be nationally, if not internationally, recognised and accredited. This would give interpreters a portable qualification that they can use anywhere within the area of recognition. If the assessment is internationally recognised, it provides the interpreter with the benefits of being able to practise within the countries in which their languages are spoken. The interpreter working in a Spanish/English combination thereby has the opportunity to work in both Spain and the UK, to improve both their languages and to keep abreast of language developments, jargon, dialects and of course any changes in the legal or health care systems.

Consistency in levels of assessment between all languages is an obvious requirement. There are clear ethical and practical implications if grade criteria are set lower in one language than another in the same examination, for example, if French is marked at a higher level than Finnish or Urdu at a higher level than sign language. The materials used must be based on real situations and texts.

Those setting assessments and those acting as oral examiners and markers of written work must be cautiously selected from graduate native speakers of their language who are also experienced interpreters. As is the case for any examiners, they have to undergo careful preparation and training in order to carry out their duties so that they have a firm grasp of not only the marking systems but also of the principles underpinning each element in them. They must obviously observe a code of conduct that includes impartiality and confidentiality, and examination boards may require a signed statement to that effect. An examination moderator is appointed to moderate consistency of both the preparation of papers and of marking. Independent accreditation of examination systems is required of examination boards, for example in the UK, to ensure their efficiency and transparency.

Cost is an inevitable challenge. Realistic costing has to reflect reasonable fees for examiners, setters and markers against what candidates can afford. Once matters become established, examination fees may be seen as an investment against future earnings.

In what follows, we look at the assessments at four different levels: access, initial professional level, postgraduate level and continuing professional development.

Access courses and assessment

Given the likely starting points described above, at the access stage there is a need to provide a firm and almost equal written and spoken base in the two languages within the general public service context as well as an insight into the nature and relationship between languages and different communication conventions. This level is attainable by the greatest number of people.

It is also important for access students, some of whom have not had an opportunity for recent study, to learn how to learn, how to evaluate their own language skills and how to make sense of their own bilingual and bicultural processes. Where such courses have been held, they have been most successful if they are multi-purpose. They not only prepare students to begin interpreter training but also to function more effectively within their own bilingual communities and to take on employment where their level of bilingualism is appropriate such as nursery and reception work.

As an example, the design of assessments at this level in the UK was originally based upon the tasks the students identified as being common demands made upon them in their daily lives (see the Certificate in Bilingual Skills offered by the Institute of Linguists Educational Trust, www.iol.org.uk/qualifications). Four tasks are assessed, using practical examples:

- Two short role plays, one in each language. For example, the candidates hold a conversation with their 'grandmother' about her need for a change in housing to accommodate her mobility problems. The candidates then go to 'a housing officer' to explain what is needed and find out what can be done. This task assesses, in both languages, listening, comprehension, speaking, information analysis and linguistic conventions such as how particular individuals are addressed, and the order and style in which information is given and negotiated.
- Sight translations, both ways, of short, straightforward texts of about 100 words. This is sometimes said to be a difficult exercise at this level, but students insist that they are often called upon to sight translate such texts as gas bills or letters asking for doctor's appointments. It does test the candidates' potential ability to transfer between languages.
- Two letters (one in each language). Stimuli are provided in the form of a series of bullet points of information to be incorporated into a well-written letter that observes the appropriate cultural conventions of the language.
- Short translation (one into each language) of relatively simple texts, such as notices about refuse collection or school reports and letters from parents about sports day.

These are unpretentious, workmanlike assessments but challenging nonetheless.

Assessment at initial professional level

It is generally recognised that the minimum standard of language skills required to ensure reliable transfer of meaning between languages equates in academic terms to a good honours degree, in level if not in breadth. It is also generally accepted that, in any profession, the possession of the first professional qualification is a first step rather than the last. All experienced teachers, lawyers or doctors are likely to be acutely conscious of the difference in the quality and depth of their existing expertise and what they possessed when they completed their first degree.

That first qualification is, however, the basis on which the rest is built. It needs to have the breadth, strength and integrity to act as a foundation. The form of assessments vary but the following assessment tasks form the core and all are based within a realistic public service context:

- two-way consecutive for dialogue e.g. an interpreted role play between a mother and a member of the health care staff discussing the advantages and disadvantages of immunisation
- simultaneous (whispered) for monologues e.g. an interpreted role play between a doctor and a patient where an elderly patient gives vent at length to her feelings about being admitted to a nursing home, or a nurse explains about weaning babies; the interpreter should be able to do this in both language directions
- translation both ways, for example the instructions for administering a medication and the potential side effects and a letter from a doctor in another country about a patient
- sight translation both ways, for example a short letter from a patient to a doctor giving the reasons for requesting another appointment and a short information text about dietary requirements.

Mark sheets include the usual criteria such as accuracy, fluency, choice of lexis, cultural accommodation, style, choice of register, voice, presentation, professionalism and co-ordination of communication, for example through interventions. The marking may also accommodate the professional dimension in that, for example, candidates may be failed outright if they make an error that would result in grave consequences, such as misinterpreting or mistranslating the dosage of a medication.

All the material should be based upon real life situations. In some countries, the domains are specific. In the UK, for example, the examination leading to the Diploma in Public Service Interpreting (DPSI), (www.iol. org.uk/qualifications) can be taken in specialised domain options of legal, health and local authority services. The last includes education welfare, housing, environmental health and social services. This allows students to study one domain in depth, part-time over an academic year. Many will study for all options over time. It would clearly be better for some students, if funds were available, to be in a position to attend longer, full-time courses and be equipped to work in all domains immediately.

Postgraduate assessments

While few are currently available, it is envisaged that at some point more professional postgraduate courses for public service interpreters will be established. These would focus on giving a valuable academic underpinning and understanding to professional practice. It is anticipated that there will be two main strands to such training: the first aimed at improving the quality of existing practitioner skills and understanding e.g. through practice-based research projects; the second at enabling participants with existing high-level language skills to acquire professional competences in interpreting and translation in the public service context. In addition to practice-based modules, there would be a range of optional study modules such as aspects of linguistics, interpreting and translation theory.

Assessment would focus on an advanced level of interpreting and translation skills, formal examination of core subjects and dissertations on a chosen area of study.

Continuing professional development (CPD) assessments

Increasingly, as in all professions, employers and colleagues are seeking formal objective evidence of skills development in terms of evidence of current best practice, specialist experience and higher levels of expertise.

Lawyers, doctors, nurses and so on are obliged, for very good reason, to show that they are keeping abreast of professional developments. Patients would not wish to consult doctors who had not practised or updated their medical knowledge since they passed their examinations ten years earlier, or to undergo neurosurgery performed by someone without specialist training. In the public services, interpreters, like other public service professionals, should also have to continue to give objective proof of current competence in terms of both level of skills and the specialist expertise acquired.

CPD assessments – where such opportunities exist – are in the process of development but a shape is beginning to emerge of portfolios describing study and attendance at lectures and conferences, combined with on-the-job assessments carried out by senior colleagues working against consistent guidelines and criteria. It may be that CPD assessments could be expanded to form an alternative incremental route to the equivalent of professionally oriented Masters programmes.

Trainers and educators of public service interpreters

Who then is going to lead successions of students from their starting points to being fully fledged, confident practitioners? Trainers are the vital ingredients in the process of development and for the future. They must not only train their students in practical skills but also educate them, in the true sense of the word, in personal and professional growth.

As in the teaching of conference interpreting and of translation, senior practitioners have a core role to play. Specialist trainers are needed with the necessary interpreting and translation skills and also the potential for developing good pedagogical skills; postgraduate courses are now being set up to train trainers, for example, at the University of Middlesex, UK.

The course content modules recommended by the EU projects for legal interpreting and translating, such as AEQUITAS (Hertog, 2000), comprise the following modules:

- educational theory to provide a knowledge of the theories of education and an understanding of the various pedagogical approaches and teaching strategies, as well as insights into cognitive and linguistic processes
- methodology to develop such skills as course designing, lesson planning, creating appropriate teaching materials, classroom management and strategies for quality assurance
- teaching practice to provide supported practical classroom experience
- management skills to aid organisation of courses, students and staff as well as record keeping, budgeting and the necessary liaison with the educational administration and colleagues.

As trainers' courses develop, so do the structures to enable trainers to keep in touch with each other, to share training materials and methods and to provide mutual support.

Graduates of such courses are the lead trainers who should be equipped to organise and design courses for the future, and to select and lead teaching teams. The rest of a teaching team comprises mainly language tutors and those who instruct the students in what they need to know about the relevant public services.

Language tutors are needed at every level. Classes of students with only one language combination are rare. Out of a class of twelve students, there may be at least three sets of language combinations and it is unlikely that the principal trainer will speak all of them. Language tutors help enhance skills in specific languages.

Instruction about public service structures and procedures are usually best done by practitioners from the relevant services. For example, a lawyer or police officer can best explain the definitions and differences between 'common assault', 'actual bodily harm' and 'grievous bodily harm' and between 'theft', 'robbery' and 'burglary'; the procedures involved in each stage of the legal process and also any forms to be filled in for each procedure. It is true that this often starts out as a reluctant participation because of other time and resource demands on a public service, before its importance to the service becomes recognised.

Teaching teams can take some time to assemble, but once created learn to complement one another's contributions and fine-tune their own under the leadership of the public service interpreter trainer. For example, contrastive work in different legal systems and their terminologies led by the language tutors can follow on after police officers and lawyers have explained investigative procedures. Both sets of trainers may be involved in the subsequent training role plays, as well as the interpreter trainer.

Selection of students for interpreter training at initial professional level

Conference interpreters and professional translators, as well as students in those disciplines, will be entirely familiar with the importance of careful selection. Inappropriate selection is likely to result in unhappiness of individual students, tutors and classmates, as well as potentially bad examination results. There is an element of professional instinct about knowing who would thrive in one's own profession, but that instinct has to be underpinned by a transparent, objective and logical process of evaluation and reflect the needs of the workplace. Evidence has to be available to resist the pressure to fill places, to cover the need for interpreters in particular languages and, most importantly, to explain to unsuccessful candidates the reasons for their lack of success. It has to be borne in mind that candidates who are originally unsuccessful may, after some remedial work, be ready for a subsequent course. Languages not covered in one course can be addressed in the following year or by colleagues elsewhere. The data collecting systems suggested in Chapter 8 would promote national coverage of the language combinations required over-all, through negotiation between course organisers.

Those who have undergone the selection process in other language-based disciplines will appreciate the need for an approach which is both rigorous and also respectful of their feelings. This sensitivity is all the more important where assessment of language skills and of personal worth may not be easily separated, where candidates are new arrivals to the country and where the language skills which they do possess may be their only credentials for meaningful employment.

Approaches to selection which risk the loss of face by individuals within their own language community should be avoided, particularly where community leaders are involved. The more successful approaches have involved consultation with the other-language speaking commu-nities from the outset to explain the course, the context, the skills required and why they are required, and to discuss the idea that not being suitable for interpreter training may simply mean that someone is better suited to some other training.

Public service interpreters are at the interface between the relevant language communities and the public services. They need the trust and respect of both. The initial interview, which forms part of the selection process, can also be the moment to introduce the concepts and reason-ing around the code of ethics of the practitioner whereby, once quali-fied, interpreters will be impartial and respect confidences. This will begin the process of disseminating ideas such as why other members of the language community cannot expect interpreters to answer personal questions about interpreting clients.

While courses are normally publicly advertised, it can also be the case that language communities will suggest suitable candidates for the selection process and provide encouragement and linguistic support.

Obviously, the relevant public services should also be involved in the initial stages of setting up courses, e.g. to advise on choice of languages to be offered at the outset so that they may be prepared to contribute to the training and to employ qualified interpreters appropriately. An invest-ment by course trainers in the local context and collaborations at an early stage is different from that in other branches of the language profession. Universities considering offering public service interpreting courses may think this outside their remit. But groundwork has already been done relating to traditional areas of training. Thanks to the founding members of AIIC and other professional language bodies, delegates at international conferences, for example, now better understand the role of the interpreter and the translator, and know, in general terms, what to expect of them. Preparation of the broader context in this new setting of PSI provides a fruitful basis for growth, and the effort needed to put into it should diminish over time as it becomes established.

Selection criteria for interpreter training at initial professional level

These normally include, as may be expected:

- Language competence: graduate level or equivalent (spoken and written) in both languages, range of registers and domains
- Interpreting potential: voice, presentation, ability to transfer between languages, interpersonal skills
- Learning potential: ability to analyse information logically, curiosity, interest in the subject
- Professional potential: maturity (not necessarily associated with chronological age), organisational abilities, availability.

The demands of the training process and the workplace have also to be taken into account. For example, the number of students in each language group must support exercises in interpreting practice. For example, there will need to be at least three or four participants with the same language combination in order to accommodate role plays and terminology-based activities. And the demand for qualified PSIs in particular language pairs should be matched with the distribution of applicants selected. Institutions within a geographical region can usefully co-ordinate the languages they include in order to provide regional coverage of both the main and less called-for language combinations.

Selection process

The following have been found to be helpful in training courses in the UK in supporting the selection of appropriate candidates:

- an application form that includes, in simple terms, a self-assessment of written and spoken competence in both languages (good/fairly good), any qualifications from any country and any previous relevant experience
- formal aptitude tests through non-technical, short role plays and short sight translations and written translations into both languages.

Agreed mark-sheets should be used and the level to be determined against the target levels and the length of the course.

- interviews by graduate-level speakers of both the languages in question
- a written text in both languages of some 200 words on subjects such as 'why I want to be a public service interpreter' or 'my previous interpreting experience', both of which can be revealing. These can be sent in with the application forms to provide a basis for consideration.

Selectors

Clearly those conducting the selection process should, wherever possible, include qualified and experienced public service interpreters working in the relevant language combinations. If a course is locally based, consideration might also be given to inviting selectors from outside the local area to help pre-empt suggestions of partiality, although involvement of the course trainers is essential too so that they can spot strengths and weakness of individuals, balance the class group learning and social dynamic and, if necessary, live with their mistakes. Language selectors from outside interpreting circles can be used, under the guidance of the trained trainer, to help judge whether, for instance, remediation is feasible in order to achieve appropriate levels of linguistic proficiency.

Information giving

Candidates need to know, well in advance of the course, what they are committing themselves to, so that they can make decisions on an informed basis. They need to know, for example, the length and general content of the course, where it will take place and when, how much home study will be expected and the qualifications of their tutors. Moreover, they need to be clear about employment arrangements and any career prospects if they qualify. For example, legal interpreters are usually freelance and it cannot be predicted how many people, speaking their language, will be arrested, witness a crime or be victims of crime. But, if they are to be called, they should know what the working arrangements are – including fees.

Training at initial professional level – approach, course design and content

Approach

There are three particular factors to be taken into account. The first is the multicultural classroom comprising students from a range of educational and national backgrounds, a familiar situation in many language class-rooms. Students may come from educational traditions where facts are learnt by rote and teacher is an authority figure, or from a tradition where students are encouraged to challenge the tutor's arguments. Some trainers have successfully used class contracts, which set out agreed expectations for the class and the tutor at the beginning of the course. Such contracts can include simple factors such as completing and sub-mitting home study assignments on time, listening thoughtfully, giving space and support to others. It is one of those valuable exercises where it is not so much the contract itself that is crucial but the discussion that precedes it.

The second factor is the prior educational experience of the students. Many will be mature people who have not studied for some time. Many will not have had the opportunity to enjoy much formal study. Many may have to learn how to learn and how to be responsible for their own skills acquisition. It may be useful to teach formally, to remind students or to introduce them to the strategies for profiling their own personal skill sets at any given moment, to measure these against the target skills sets, to identify how they learn best and to organise their own incre-mental development within the structure of the course. In doing so, stu-dents then identify what help they need and where that help might best be found. It is obviously beneficial to share such ongoing profiles with tutors and even, from time to time, to collaborate on them with fellow students.

The third factor is increasingly common for all students. It is no longer necessarily the case that the typical student in tertiary education is a sin-gle young person, undistracted by any other responsibilities. It is often more common for students to have other commitments such as paid work, families, extended families and community duties. This is proba-bly the case for nearly all public service interpreter students. In addition, and especially if they are new arrivals, they are obliged to spend more time on the mechanics of daily life while they are establishing them-selves. In normal academic circumstances, the students' personal lives are not the business of the tutors except when involved in a pastoral role. Nor is it the business of the public service interpreter trainer, unless the students offer to share information. Nonetheless, and especially in cultures where boundaries between work and private life are less marked, the tutors are likely to become aware of more dimensions of their stu-dents' lives. Tutors have found it helpful to set aside time and space and to consider, and agree among themselves in advance, the unwritten rules they are going to observe in terms of keeping confidences and what, if any, distance they might wish to keep. Without that prior thought, tutors have found themselves initially overtaxed by subtle demands on their time which they had not anticipated. In overtly accommodating the whole student, where appropriate, the tutors educate in the true sense of the word and produce more rounded and confident interpreters. Indeed, public service interpreter students are often new arrivals or, as in the case of students originally from South Africa, have had tough life experiences. Whether one thinks it appropriate or not, during this training there may be moments when old, unresolved situations are recalled. When bereavement and the breaking of bad news are being discussed, for example, the responses to deaths of relatives when there had been no opportunity to grieve, may revive and have to be accommodated. Immigration interviews, with all the necessary exploration of evidence of fear or torture or intimidation may have similar consequences. Students have to be supported through this, perhaps by a trained counsellor, if they are going to interpret in similar situations.

Course design and content

The central course content is usually approached through the chosen domain. So, for example, there can be a series of domain units in the medical field to cover the main areas of work such as antenatal care and childbirth, through paediatrics, gynaecology, urology, cardiology, surgery, infectious diseases and geriatrics. The domain units in local government services will include such areas as social services, educational welfare, housing and environmental health. The legal services domain units will include police procedures such as investigation and arrest, the various courts and tribunals and the implementation of sentencing, as well as civil matters. Within each of these domain units, the five 'golden threads' described below are interwoven.

The domain unit about antenatal care provides a useful short illustration for these five 'threads' which are gradually interwoven to form an ever stronger skein of skills. The significance behind seemingly routine antenatal appointments should be borne in mind: questions such as whether there is a higher infant and maternal mortality rate among other-language speakers than in the majority populations needs to be empirically researched. A proportion of these patients may not, in the past, have had adequate medical care, nutrition or accurate information about pregnancy and childbirth; the risk of complications can therefore be higher. Last but not least, these young women may not have their own mothers and extended family members around to give them support.

1 The structure, purposes, procedures, processes and personnel of services involved in antenatal care

Conference and business interpreters normally have forewarning of assignments, so that they can do some preparatory research on the subject and its terminology. On the whole, public service interpreters do not. They therefore have to have a solid background understanding of the public services they are going to work in, so that they can interpret reliably at very short notice. This does not mean that students should, or could, be expected to have an in-depth knowledge of law or medicine but that they should acquire a functional basis and, just as importantly, the strategies for building on that basis by retrieving and recording information with each assignment.

A domain unit on antenatal care is best introduced by a doctor or midwife and followed by observation visits to antenatal clinics in hospitals and doctors' surgeries, and sometimes to homes, obviously subject to the consent of staff and patients. Observation visits are carefully prepared to help focus students' attention on relevant matters, and observation sheets can usefully be devised in advance to note procedures and terminology. Students should also be aware of the different types of personnel involved in the service delivery; for example, in the health service midwives, radiographers and dieticians, their responsibilities, accountability and even uniforms.

As noted earlier, practical issues cannot be ignored. Notes are made about, for example, the geography of the clinic, how best to get there, where to park and what security measures have to be observed. Public service interpreters are expected to arrive in good time and in good order. Professional contact is made with health care staff so that, once qualified, students know whom to telephone for elucidation of an unfamiliar technical term or procedure, for example, points for discussion include the preferred gender for interpreting assignments. Clearly, a female interpreter is preferred in an antenatal clinic and a male interpreter for men's urology. Nevertheless, in an emergency and when there is no other option, an interpreter of either gender should be able to handle the matter sensitively. There have been occasions when a woman went into sudden labour with complications and the only interpreter nearby was male. There are, after all, male doctors and midwives.

2 Domain-specific vocabulary

Technical terminology is used when health care staff discuss a patient between themselves, expert-to-expert. It is rarely used in conversations between health care workers and pregnant mothers beyond such words as may be considered to be generally understood such as a 'scan' and even 'amniocentesis'. The linguistic challenge is the use of euphemisms used to overcome embarrassments, or simply because the patient does not know the formal term for, for example, 'uterus', 'vulva' or 'cervix'. Informal words and phrases are used such as 'down there', 'my private parts'.

A first useful step is an introduction to terminology in each language by the language tutors, based on, for example, a set of simple anatomical diagrams of the female abdomen at various stages of pregnancy. (Video and DVD material about the development of a foetus and such like can also be used, if available). Both the formal nomenclature and the range of the informal terms should be covered in both languages. It may become evident that some students are not familiar with basic anatomy and the mechanics of childbirth, but, as interpreters, their accurate knowledge is essential.

Students can be given lists of terms which they can add to their personal glossaries, either in paper form as small loose-leaf ring binders or stored electronically in a database of some kind on a hand-held computer that stays with them throughout their training and practice. Glossaries are constantly being extended and updated. Additionally, students should be encouraged to store telephone numbers, useful website addresses and up to date procedural information. The glossaries provide an essential quick source of reference if, for example, the interpreter has been working in another part of the health care service and needs a reminder. Students will take advice from their language tutors in how to set these out. Glossaries and other databases and file notes should not include confidential information in case they are lost.

3 Interpreting techniques and translation

Actual interpreting training largely takes place through role plays. Armed with their understanding of the domain, the procedures and processes of the interpreting environment – here, antenatal care – and the terminology of the relevant domain, students are taken through simulated interpreting situations of graded difficulty. Relevant public service staff are encouraged to participate and play themselves in the role plays. One student acts as interpreter and another, in the same language group, acts as the pregnant mother or perhaps the father of the baby. The health care worker and 'patient' are given prompt notes.

At the simplest, these role plays may be not more than: 'Mrs A is visiting the clinic for the first time to have her pregnancy confirmed and to register her details'. An intermediate-level role-play task may involve Mrs B having a scan. Explanations will be given to Mrs A before and during the procedure and her questions answered. An advanced task could involve Mrs C and Mr C, and even an older family member, in a sensitive discussion about, for example, suspected abnormalities.

Afterwards, there is a class evaluation or 'critique'. Part of the class contract, described above, looks at how students should support one another. The ability to provide objective comments to colleagues on their performance and to evaluate one's own performance is a component part of ongoing professional life: to affirm the good, to suggest improvements and to challenge the unacceptable. Post role-play critiques usually start with the student interpreter evaluating their own performance, the health care workers evaluating their own performance in the way they worked with the interpreter and across cultures, the 'patient' reflecting on how they found the experience – and then the class as a whole. Critique sheets may be distributed to focus discussion.

For lower level tasks, the critique sheet may refer to no more than the interpreter's accuracy, voice and basic interpreting technique. At higher levels the critique criteria may include style, professional presentation, problem-solving and dealing with multiple interlocutors (see below for a more comprehensive list).

Both the students and the public service personnel become adept at role-playing different situations, in recognising levels of linguistic difficulty and, in the more advanced level tasks, in taking mischievous delight in stretching the challenges for all concerned. Aggressive fathers-to-be, weeping mothers-to-be, X-ray technicians with strong regional dialects and grannies with genetic secrets to hide emerge on stage without much warning – but in the sure and certain knowledge that their fellow students will find similar or worse challenges ahead. It is, at best, a form of intellectual professional athletics that will stand them in good stead when they enter the workplace.

In the process, the student interpreters are learning, among other things, how language is used differently by different generations and sexes; the significance of pauses, incomplete sentences and turn taking. They learn to follow precisely and invisibly in the footprints of the speaker. They gain the confidence to retain control of the communication by, where necessary for example, pointing to the speaker they are interpreting for to prevent that speaker from being talked over; to pre-empt potential chaotic communication where people are all shouting at once or an imbalance in the communication where the quiet individual never gets heard. At the same time they leave the content of the communication to those participating in it.

Critique sheets can expand accordingly to include:

- accuracy
- register
- style
- fluency
- voice
- professionalism and presentation
- dealing with technical terms
- cultural mediation – in the linguistic sense
- consecutive interpreting
- whispered simultaneous (and when)
- handling the communication process e.g. turn-taking
- observation of code of ethics e.g. making interpreter interventions appropriately
- note-taking.

Apart from role plays, the usual drills and exercises are used that are familiar to interpreters in any branch of the profession. Short-term memory and listening comprehension are improved. Note-taking and voice exercises are practised.

Factors that are not always part of the experience of other branches of the profession are also tackled. Where, for example, do interpreters position themselves while the patient is being examined by the doctor or having a scan? What precautions should they take if the patient has AIDS? How do they don, and dispose of, gowns and gloves and/or interpret wearing a surgical mask?

During the training course students should be given the experience of telephone and videoconference interpreting (see Kelly 2007; Connell 2006 and Braun 2007 respectively). Both have certain disadvantages when compared with face-to-face interpreting, and students should be aware of what those are so that they know which approach is appropriate to which situation. These technologies are more commonly used in countries where distance and climate inhibit the organisation of face-to-face meetings but may also be attractive to managers for budgetary and logistical reasons. The expertise of the interpreter is crucial in monitoring the appropriateness of the technology to the situation.

Instruction in the relevant academic theory underpinning interpreting as a cognitive activity and social practice takes place as part of the learning experience. Good foundations laid at initial professional level prepare students for making sense of what they do and why, in ways that allow them to explore theory in greater depth later, as well as to reflect on their own practice.

Translation competence is also covered at a foundation level to enable students to deal reliably with short, straightforward texts that they might come across in a normal day such as housing application and benefit forms. Suffice it to say at this point that there is rarely a public service event without a related piece of written text.

4   Code of ethics and guidelines to good practice

These have already been discussed in Chapter 3 (cf. also Chapter 5) and form an integral part of all components of PSI training. In a unit such as the one on the antenatal domain used here as an illustration, discussions would include the implications of confidentiality and the reasons why that is so important – not only in routine matters but also in relation to confidences about, for example, the paternity of a child.

Impartiality is also essential, regardless of the personalities involved. The interventions, properly handled, should enable the interpreter to collaborate in keeping the cultural and linguistic balls 'in court'. But what does the interpreter do when ethical issues arise, e.g. if he or she knows or suspects something which has a salient bearing on the health of the child or the mother? Under English law, for example, anyone is obliged to report suspected child-abuse to the appropriate authorities within the shortest possible time. But what does the interpreter do about less clear-cut issues where, for example, alternative medicines may have been taken which may contraindicate other medication given by the clinic?

One approach to teaching ethics is to divide the class into imaginary disciplinary panels, provide them with hypothetical scenarios and then to invite them to make decisions on whether the codes have been breached and, if so, what sanctions should be applied. The scenarios have to be carefully prepared and can range from persistent lateness to deliberate negligence. It is a useful exercise although, oddly, students tend to be more severe in their sanctions sometimes than more experienced interpreters.

The implementation of codes and good practice guidelines also includes training interpreters how to conduct their professional arrangements appropriately. A firm grasp of seemingly mundane factors is essential, such as diary management, how and when to accept an assignment, invoicing and proper record-keeping including in relation to tax matters.

It is best for students to think these factors through in the classroom, to be clear about the parameters and to know what the available strategies might be for problem-solving. Once on an assignment, they are on their own and irreversible decisions can be made very quickly.

5 **Continuing personal and professional development**

Students are taught the strategies for being responsible for their own development within the classroom and how that should continue after qualification. Professional development includes profiling one's own needs and learning from each assignment and storing that information appropriately, for example, terminology, as we have seen; attending relevant lectures and conferences and reading and simply talking and listening to well-informed people. These strategies are common to all language professionals and probably differ only in content.

Personal development is, however, perhaps more important where interpreters come in contact daily with the events and experiences of the public services. There is a need to avoid hardening emotional responses and to absorb and learn from these experiences so that the job can be done better next time. Interpreters need to retain their sensitivities, rather than blunt them. Sobbing over the patient is rarely helpful but feelings should be dealt with properly afterwards, lest they impede future assignments. The other disciplines within the public services, such as doctors, nurses and police officers, face the same personal demands and have established relatively effective methods of dealing with them. This often includes no more than talking to each other – more difficult for the interpreter acting alone.

Possible strategies for the interpreter include talking to colleagues who are within the circle of confidentiality. This includes interpreters' mentors and supervisors, who will understand the linguistic challenges, and/or the appropriate health care staff who are clear about the reason for the discussion and know how best to handle it. In the event of a really demanding event, such as a multiple fatal traffic accident, the other public service disciplines are likely to allow the interpreter to use their post-traumatic counselling services where these exist.

These five threads are developed through each domain unit so that they can be called upon automatically and intuitively whether on the hard shoulder of the motorway or in the housing office.

The first two elements, knowledge of the service and extension of vocabulary knowledge, can be done partly through distance learning but the last three have to be done mainly face-to-face. Learning and practising the techniques of interpreting and discussing the implementation of codes and good professional practice are interactive processes of education as well as training. Experience has shown that, given careful selection, it takes a minimum of 150 hours contact time plus home study time to prepare students with adequate existing bilingual and related skills to work in one set of services, for example law or health care i.e. to reach initial professional level. Teaching can be offered on a full-time basis, or, if sufficient time is allowed for reflection, part-time or in blocks.

Towards the end of a course

All training courses tend to include what is needed to round off and finalise the experience. Preparations for an end-of-course formal examination inevitably form part of this. Mock assessments may be done a few months prior to the actual examination to allow all students time to reach the required standard.

Students should be connected to the mainstream of the wider profession they are to join after qualifying so that they are prepared for practice. This is discussed in the next chapter and many of the necessary structures are still in the process of development. Their first year of practice may cause particular anxiety. They will need the familiar faces of the public service personnel and the senior public service interpreters they have met during their training and most of all, they need each other.

Training and education at postgraduate level

Ideally, the specific training of public service interpreters and translators should *begin* at a postgraduate level, for instance, after the completion of a first degree in languages or in a subject related to the relevant fields in the public services with language expertise acquired through personal circumstances. It is, however, rarely the case that PSIT (Public Service Interpreting and Translating) training starts at this level, but this is a longer term goal and some initiatives at this level are beginning to emerge.

So what follows are some suggestions for consideration, assuming as a starting point existing qualifications equivalent, in academic terms, to a good first degree. While there may be some potential students primarily undertaking study out of academic interest, the majority of students are likely to be individuals who are qualified to bachelors level, have some experience in the profession and are seeking to develop their skills and understanding of practice. However, unless there are subsidies from the state or elsewhere, it is unlikely that many public service interpreters and translators will be in a position to afford significant fees for courses and examinations. Part-time modularised courses with modest fees are likely to be needed for the foreseeable future.

Course tutors should be familiar with the public service context, although not all need the same level and type of experience and different perspectives may be covered. In other words, not all tutors should be senior PSITs. Following the model of some existing masters programmes in translation and interpreting, a team of experienced practitioners, academics and subject field experts is likely to provide an optimum mix for a qualification at this level. Tutors from related fields such as senior interpreters and translators from other contexts, applied linguists, forensic linguists and sociolinguists, as well as visiting lecturers from the public service arena such as lawyers or medical anthropologists have much to offer on PSIT programmes. In addition to subject knowledge and expertise, practitioner tutors will need the pedagogic skills to support students through skill development and an educational process of making sense of their own practice in a complex, and often difficult, area, taking them forward to high levels of professional maturity.

The incremental process of training and education should never stop in any profession. CPD courses are now offered by professional associations, universities and many other bodies. While not all the stages in that process may be conducted within formal structures, some formal structures are useful to demonstrate proven achievement of professional development. These are useful not only to the individuals concerned but also to clients who wish to engage them. In addition, this formal process enables the body of knowledge to grow, expand and keep up to date in ways that can be evaluated against recognised criteria, recorded and disseminated.

Whether those formal structures are academic or professional will depend to some extent on national conventions. Masters programmes may prioritise the practice and theory components in different ways depending on the learning outcomes which are envisaged. Such differentiation is already common in many established translation programmes in particular. A further possibility is for universities to offer subsets of the full range of modules with a particular focus on practice, leading to a postgraduate certificate rather than a masters degree.

Another possible way forward is to combine different routes, including, for instance, a university-based programme (or selected modules) and specified formal CPD modules. It should be mentioned here that CPD is only recently becoming a mandatory requirement for registration with professional bodies. Its current format leaves much of the responsibility to the individual practitioners in terms of profiling their own skills against what they need for their careers, and for then seeking out what additional training and experience they need in order to fill the gaps. There are currently plans emerging for formalising and facilitating that process, when resources become available, through the provision of more training in specialised areas, augmented by supervised practice.

The general principles of assessment are described earlier in this chapter. The design, content and number of study modules comprising a full programme of study should align with postgraduate study in other fields and offer opportunities for credit transfer in the normal way. The facility for *international* credit transfer, enabling students to study in the countries of both their working languages, would be particularly useful.

Core modules on a postgraduate PSIT programme could include the following: Consecutive and simultaneous (chuchotage) interpreting practice working towards specific settings, an overview of interpreting studies, translation in the public services (practice), an overview of institutional settings and terminology studies. Optional modules could include management of other PSITs, mentoring and support, supervision, evaluation and topics of special interest such as interpreting in cross examinations in court hearings, the translation of psychiatric reports, strategies for cost-effective delivery of PSIT, interpreting in domestic conflict or serious fraud and interpreting in situations involving children.

Suggested activities

- observe a court hearing and identify what procedures, terminology and interpreting techniques would need to be known in order to interpret well in that situation
- design a lesson plan to teach the terminology involved
- design a CPD assessment for medical interpreters wishing to affirm their skills in the domain of oncology – and cost it
- profile personal skills against those needed to interpret in the public service context.

Further reading

Baker, C. (1996) *Foundations of Bilingual Education and Bilingualism* (2nd edition). Clevedon: Multilingual Matters.

Bell, S. (1997) 'The challenges of setting and monitoring the standards of community interpreting: An Australian perspective', in A. Carr, R. Roberts, A. Dufour and D. Steyn (eds) *The Critical Link 1. Interpreters in the Community.* Amsterdam: John Benjamins 93–107.

Cambridge, J. (1999) 'Information Loss in Bilingual Medical Interviews through an Untrained Interpreter', *The Translator* 5(2): 201–19.

Gentile, A., Ozolins, U. and Vasilakakos, M. (1996) *Liaison Interpreting.* Melbourne: University Press.

Erik Hertog, and Bart v.d. Beer (eds) (2006) *Taking Stock: Research and Methodology in Community Interpreting. Linguistica Antverpiensia New Series* 5. Antwerp: Hoger Instituut voor Vertalers en Tolken.

I. Mason (ed.) (1999) *Dialogue Interpreting.* Special issue of *The Translator* 05, 2.

I. Mason (ed.) (2001) *Triadic Exchanges, Studies in Dialogue Interpreting.* Manchester: St Jerome.

Niska, H. (2002) 'Community interpreter training. Present, past, future', in G. Garzone and M. Viezzi (eds) *Interpreting in the 21st Century.* Amsterdam: John Benjamins. 133–44.

Penney, C. and Sammons, S. (1997) 'Training the community interpreter: the Nunavut Arctic College experience', in A. Carr, R. Roberts, A. Dufour and D. Steyn (eds) *The Critical Link 1. Interpreters in the Community.* Amsterdam: John Benjamins. 65–76.

Pöchhacker, F. (2004) *Introducing Interpreting Studies.* London: Routledge.

Roberts, R. (2000) 'Interpreter assessment tools for different settings', in R. Roberts, S. Carr, D. Abraham and A. Dufour (eds) *The Critical Link 2: Interpreters in the Community.* Amsterdam: John Benjamins. 103–20.

Romaine, S. (1995) *Bilingualism.* (2nd edition). Oxford: Basil Blackwell.

C. Roy (ed.) (2000) *Innovative Practices for Teaching Sign Language Interpreters.* Washington DC: Galludet University Press.

Wadensjö, C. (1998) *Interpreting as Interaction.* London: Longman.

5
Establishing a Professional Framework

Once trained and qualified, public service interpreters need a professional structure within which to practise. This structure is still under construction in many countries but the principal elements are emerging. There is a growing international similarity of outcomes, even though progress is taking place at different speeds, with different priorities and is subject to different national systems and conventions.

There is often confusion as to what a profession is. A class of students of public service interpreting was once asked to define the meaning of a profession. Alarmingly, one said, 'they can charge higher fees'. Another offered, 'service with a smile'.

A deeper understanding of professions and professionalism is the cornerstone of training public service interpreters and translators. As already noted, students come from a variety of cultural backgrounds and from different generations. It is essential that they all share a common grasp of the structures and the underlying principles that should govern their learning and practice so that they can share in the professional development process, and that clients from any language group are equally clear as to what those structures and principles are.

That development process is taking place against a background of change throughout the language professions. Increasing globalisation of trade and industry, of the arts and the movement of people between countries for education, business and tourism is placing a significant demand upon the skills of professional linguists. The notion that there is a global use of English can be misleading. Firstly, the use of English as a *lingua franca* does not necessarily reflect the cultural backgrounds of its speakers. A former German chancellor is reported to have said: 'We sell in English but we buy in German' and his comments may not only be based upon his pride in his own language but also upon a recognition of the need for a deeper understanding of what is being negotiated to meet the needs of the German customers. Secondly, an adequate command of non-mother tongue English[1] is usually limited to those who have had the educational opportunities to learn it and the professional need to use it or, as in the case of eastern European countries for example, those who use it as a third or even fourth language.

Language skills are beginning to be seen as a primary, rather than secondary, prerequisite for a range of essential activities. As a consequence, both employers and professional linguists are beginning to require more specific benchmarks of language competence and a clearer contextual framework. Otherwise, unless there is always someone else in a position to judge linguistic competence, there is the potential for those with inadequate or unsuitable language skills to be employed. There is a risk that, without some form of coherent framework, professionally trained and qualified linguists will be ill-equipped to protect themselves or their expertise.

The professional approaches being adopted by public service interpreters and translators, in response to their own working context, are contributing to a broader debate over the traditional conventions of the more established branches of the translation and interpreting professions. Qualified interpreters and translators rightly think of themselves as professionals in so far as they observe a code of conduct that includes *inter alia* accuracy and impartiality. While many voluntarily belong to national or international language professional bodies that require members to meet specified criteria and observe a code of conduct, it is not normally obligatory for them to do so. Consequently, some linguists working as translators and interpreters, especially those without appropriate qualifications or training, operate outside this framework.

It can be said that there are some areas of language work where such structured arrangements are less common, such as in literary translation. Here the skilled translators of novels, poetry and plays become respected on the basis of the evidence of their previous work although associations of literary translators are also highly active in many countries. It is also the case, however, that anyone who speaks two languages does some interpreting or translation during their daily lives, such as helping out a fellow customer in a shop who is in difficulties with a language or translating a letter for a friend. The same applies to medicine, in the sense that everyone takes care of sick friends and family and gives them a pill for their headache, but that is very different from making reliable diagnoses and doing surgery.

It is clear to most people when the point at which the need for a professional structure arises. This applies particularly within the public service context, where belonging to a profession usually means belonging to a formally regulated profession for very good reasons.

A definition of a formally regulated profession

The definition of a regulated profession may vary between countries and cultures. A basic definition follows.

> A profession is a group of people who share a common expertise and who *profess* to a code of conduct and values that is designed to protect their clients, their body of expertise and their colleagues in their own and associated disciplines. This goes beyond their immediate self-interest but nonetheless is in the interests of the individual members of a profession as it signals to potential clients that they have agreed to behave in a 'professional' way.

Status and trust cannot be given. They have to be earned. Regulated professions therefore establish what is needed to meet their codes of conduct in terms of national, transparent, accountable and consistent criteria for:

- selection for professional training
- initial and continuous professional training
- examinations
- accreditation
- registration
- implementing the code of conduct
- disciplinary procedures where there are allegations of breaches of the code.

The whole is underpinned by rigorous professional stewardship to give a sound financial footing to fulfil the aims – encompassed in its code – of the profession and its membership. By contrast, in business or industry the prime aim is to make a profit, and any standards and ethical considerations are implemented to achieve that aim.

Where members of a profession operate outside the public services, such as doctors in private practice and lawyers in law firms, the professional principles are still paramount. A doctor or a lawyer is always subject to the rules and codes of the profession of which he or she is a member. Part of those rules and codes are likely to contain clear guidance about the proper conduct of the business of supplying their expertise to the public.

The reasons for having a regulated professional framework in the public service context

A regulated professional framework is needed to protect clients and becomes necessary at the point where a significant level of expertise is required, where important decisions are to be taken, where skills are offered to the general public and to other professional disciplines and where fees are involved.

In the public service context everyone has to know, without asking, that all the professionals involved are competent and appropriately qualified for the task, for example, in court hearings, medical consultations and interviews with social workers. That includes the interpreters and translators who have a pivotal and responsible role where there is not a shared language. They become members of the multidisciplinary professional teams.

A formal profession arises when trust has to be engendered. Where a client is not in a position to judge the quality of service at the point of delivery, more has to be known about the competence of the provider of the service. This is especially the case where potentially irreversible actions are to be taken. One would not, for example, allow a doctor to remove one's tonsils purely on the grounds that he or she claimed to be good at the job.

A professional framework is also needed to protect the standards of the language professions from external pressures in the same way as other established professions do. The medical and legal professions, for example, would quite rightly oppose pressures for doctors and lawyers to be allowed to practise with lower standards in order to increase their numbers quickly or to provide a cheaper service. Hence, in many countries, professions jealously guard their independence from government and other potential sources of external pressure in the interests of their clients, while being open to liaising with such bodies in positive and constructive terms.

Without a unifying professional framework, public service linguists are powerless to deal with, for instance, a situation long known informally as the 'unholy trinity': clients, untrained 'suppliers' of services and some educational institutions. Clients, such as public services and governments, are often not language aware. Many representatives of these bodies assume that anyone who can speak a limited amount of another language can interpret and translate. This unfounded rationalisation encourages the employment of individuals, who possess low standards of skills and can then be paid lower fees. The second group are untrained interpreters and translators who are already working in the field and feel threatened by the notion of having their skills tested. Many of the best-qualified interpreters and translators started in just this way, but blossomed through the opportunity to expand upon and formalise their skills. The third group are educational establishments that offer courses and assessments which do not meet professional requirements, but which could, nevertheless, make a contribution to a co-ordinated incremental programme of development rather than being offered as an end in themselves.

It is also essential to protect colleagues in other disciplines. Public service activities usually involve multidisciplinary teams. For example, when a woman is in labour, midwives, doctors, haematologists, anaesthetists and paediatric nurses may all contribute. They have all been trained to work together smoothly, effectively and, if necessary, quickly without further discussion. They know each other's role and competences and expect to be able to rely on one another. Their whole attention is on the safe delivery of the baby and the well-being of the mother. They make professional decisions on the basis of their own expertise and that of their colleagues. If errors are made, their own professional reputations and careers are at stake together with the well-being of the mother and baby. They must therefore be able to trust the public service interpreters in their team. Chapter 7 describes the training colleagues in other professions need to be able to work with interpreters and translators.

A professional framework is also needed to protect interpreters and translators. They can benefit from having the backing of a professional body; from being secure in the knowledge that, if need be, they will be supported in implementing their code of conduct and good practice.

Language practitioners also occasionally need protection from each other. Anecdotal evidence abounds of occasions such as when a qualified interpreter attends a court to interpret and finds that an unqualified interpreter has been employed during the investigative process and appears to have misinterpreted vital information. As a result, the integrity of the serial communication process as well as the integrity of justice is at risk. Interpreters may indeed have cause to complain about each other, but there is a need for a proper professional process to resolve matters.

Equally important is for the professional framework to act as a central focus for internal and external communication. External communication is needed for liaison with the public services, governments, other professional bodies and the general public. No profession exists in a vacuum.

Each one has to maintain ongoing relationships outside the profession. National and even international consistency of standards and approaches have to be sought, constantly reviewed in the light of experience and change and then implemented through the national professional framework in the form of training, assessment and practice. Otherwise, there is no consistency of practice or expectations, no coherent strategy for growth and development.

For example, national standards of interpreting and translation competence are negotiated on the basis of what is needed for the tasks to be done. Therefore a thorough understanding is required of, for instance, legal cross-examinations, medical interviews and social welfare consultations that can only be gathered through the disciplines involved. National interdisciplinary strategies are needed for updating information and adapting to change. There are continuing and inevitable changes in, for instance, legislation and medical procedures. Each carries implications for terminology and processes which interpreters and translators must be made aware of. National guidelines to interdisciplinary good practice (see Chapters 3, 7 and 8) are based upon the development of conventions, which support the overall purpose – such as providing satisfactory medical care. Consultations have to take place, therefore, over when and how, for instance, the interpreter should move from consecutive to simultaneous mode; when and how they should intervene when the communication flow is being hindered and what the best arrangements are for commissioning and receiving assignments.

National interdisciplinary training guidelines (see Chapter 7) are required, so that those involved in the public services know how to work with public service translators and interpreters and *vice versa*. This will involve important matters such as establishing the fact that interpreters and translators should be called when there is no adequate shared language and also simple practical items such as why good translations cannot be completed within unrealistic timescales and where the interpreter should sit in an ambulance to do their job but not get in the way. (There is said to have been an occasion when an interpreter sat on a client's oxygen tube.)

Providing a national point of communication is therefore essential and answers the question 'who do I contact?' for information about translation and interpreting matters. If a civil servant, a government minister or a member of the public wishes to contact a central point, they need to be sure that they will receive an informed answer that, ideally, is representative of the profession as a whole. There may be one or more such reference points, taking into account any separation of function between the bodies associated with one particular profession. Medical and other professions may, for instance, according to country, have separate bodies for regulation/registration, qualifications and membership.

Providing a positive public face for the language professions helps, among other things, to educate members of the public in the professions' standards, good practice and purposes; to engage them in matters of interest and to promote a well founded image of responsibility. It appears that, in some countries, skills in a second and even third language are taken as a matter of course and in others not. Languages other than the national ones may have positive associations with foreign holidays and successful commercial enterprises, or negative associations. Either way, those language skills are often not sufficiently valued and should be publicly recognised and celebrated within an appropriate professional framework.

Internal communication within the profession is equally essential, especially as interpreters and translators are usually sole practitioners. There is, for example, a need to support the practitioner in situations which may be isolating and stressful, a not uncommon occurrence in the public services. An interpreter may deal with birth and bereavement on the same day, and need support within the circle of professional confidentiality. An internal communication framework is necessary to seek a professional consensus, to harness positive energies and to diffuse negative ones.

Also of significance is the communication among colleagues at an international level. The Critical Link international conferences, established by a group of Canadian specialists, take place every three years. These provide a focus for practitioners, trainers and academics to gather from all over the world. Informal networks enable a continuous interchange of ideas and mutual support between Critical Link conferences. The need for international consistency of standards is outlined in the paper 'Aequitas to Aequalitas: establishing standards in legal interpreting and translation in the European Union' (Hertog, Corsellis, Rasmussen, Vanden Bosch, Van der Vlis and Keijzer-Lambooy from Critical Link 4, 2007).

It is a matter for a wider debate as to whether all these factors also apply in other areas of language practice, as well as to those working in the public service domains. However, one of the significant benefits of having a properly constituted professional body is that it can apply for external funding from governments and charitable trusts to support its development process.

Establishing a professional framework: management of change

The established professions such as medicine and law took some hundreds of years to establish the structures they now have. Linguists in the public service context have to achieve the same formats in a much shorter time, if they are to meet the pressing need that has arisen as a result of contemporary movements of people.

It has to be accepted, however, that a regulated profession cannot be established overnight. Sufficient numbers of adequately qualified interpreters and translators will not be available immediately. Indeed the very qualifications themselves may not exist. It is an incremental process requiring commitment, competence, patience, vision, communication and goodwill.

Those who have gone some way to achieving what is needed have the benefit of hindsight. In these countries, the structures have usually been developed through a series of individual initiatives through opportunities that presented themselves, and working relationships formed along the way. In the light of experience and many mistakes, with hindsight, a clearer and more co-ordinated approach might be followed, including incremental stages such as the ones described below.

Recognising the realities of existing perceptions

While the development of a professional framework appears entirely sensible in principle and in the best interests of both public service interpreters and their clients, the actual implementation of such a framework can give rise to a range of anxieties and uncertainties as well as downright opposition. This can be compounded by the fact that previous loose arrangements allowed a freedom of activity that more formal structures tend to curtail, such as interpreters or translators without adequate qualifications, or none at all, being able to gain employment of a sort; asking a cousin to deal with an interpreting or translation assignment when one has something better to do; public services paying low fees because there are no benchmarks of competence; public services pressurising linguists to take on extra roles and tasks or to be partial because of the lack of a definition of role and codes. It is reported that in one hospital, for example, unqualified interpreters were asked to take medical case histories on their own.

These anxieties are real and it is not an easy task to overcome decades of unstructured activity, either on an individual basis when a professional framework which requires accredited training and qualifications is introduced or institutionally, as cash strapped public services are unlikely to welcome immediately the notion of qualified linguists able to justify reasonable fees.

Creating a central professional language body

In a large number of countries there is a professional language organisation of some sort. These range from informal groupings of working linguists to the more formal language professional bodies. Existing organisations may or may not be the right focus for a regulated, formal professional organisation for public service linguists. In addition, different countries take different approaches to professions.

Best practice suggests that the central body be non-profit making in order to establish an identity of integrity and to defend it from accusations of self-interest. Depending upon the legal structures of a country, such a body can be formed as a company with limited liability and its aims and governance clearly set out; it may or may not also have charitable status. Those involved in its establishment and organisation should primarily be individuals respected for their professional competence. They need support from all sides in order to take matters forward and to communicate, consult, collaborate with and convince the disparate parties involved.

Start up funding has been raised in a variety of ways, from charitable trusts to subsidy by existing language professional bodies. Later, once the organisation has something to offer, support comes through membership fees.

There are differences in function between membership, regulation and qualification within the overall structure of any one profession. The professional membership body comprises those eligible to join and acts as a forum for professional matters listed earlier in this chapter. The regulation body administers the professional register and disciplinary procedures. The qualification body administers professional examinations at all levels. In some of the older established professions, these three functions while interrelated, are more distinct. One of the reasons for being so is that the separate functions offer checks and balances for one another. Current trends and thinking are affecting all professions and discussions are taking place over, for example, whether and how there should be involvement in all three functions by independent outside parties and increasing appropriate transparency. It will be interesting to see how the emerging formalising language professions organise their structures over time and whether, for example, countries will start with all three interrelated distinct bodies or start with one overarching body and separate later. Possible starting points are described below (cf. Corsellis, Cambridge, Glegg and Robson 2007).

Establishing standards of linguistic and professional competence

These have been described in Chapter 3. Such standards can only be defined against the task in question and not by what most candidates can achieve on a good day.

Setting up a registration panel

A registration panel is normally made up of qualified and practising interpreters and translators but may include others who act as informed and independent arbiters. To prevent unacceptable lobbying, it may be wise to have a registration panel of some twenty senior linguists and to rotate them, so that three or four are involved in each annual or six-monthly selection meeting. The panel's function is to decide who is appropriately qualified for admission to the register, against registration criteria that are transparent and public.

Identifying registration criteria

A professional register contains the details of individuals who have reached the recognised standards of competence. A register is the central component of a profession's structure. It is not simply a list or a directory. It is the physical interface between a profession and those whom it serves. It is the profession's guarantee, so far as is humanly possible, that those whom it allows within its ranks are fit and suitable to practise.

The registration criteria include more than objective assessment of language and professional skills at an appropriate level. More is required such as security vetting. This ranges from the proof of absence of any relevant criminal records, as required for all those who work in the public services in many countries, to the higher security screening required for interpreters and translators likely to work in the context of, for example, terrorism. The former particularly excludes people who have been convicted of violence, dishonesty or child abuse. Other offences such as having taken a lower class illegal substance while a student, ten years earlier, or a single instance of being caught driving while unfit, may not be considered prohibitive. However, more than that would bring into question whether the individual was suitable for a profession where they would have dealings with vulnerable clients. The usual mechanism for acquiring security clearance is for the applicants themselves to approach the relevant authorities and then present the outcomes to the registration panel. Registrants remain under a duty to inform their register if they are subsequently convicted of a criminal offence. It is probable that members of a local community or language group will know about any convictions and that may reflect upon the register if not handled transparently.

Evidence of experience is relevant. Some registers issue logbooks to be completed, after each assignment, by the interpreter and the public service client. Such logbooks are useful, as evidence of continuing competence, where annual re-registration is required.

References should be taken up. It is a fact of life that there are people who are very good at passing examinations and in presenting themselves but who are less good on the job for a variety of reasons. References as to competence in the workplace and to character are useful. They do have their limitations but provide valuable supporting evidence if a fellow professional is prepared to put their personal reputation on the line to support a colleague's application.

Registrants must formally agree to observe the code of ethics or conduct and be subject to the associated disciplinary procedures where a breach of the code is alleged (see Chapter 3). Pretending that one did not know one's own code can be no defence.

There should also be agreement to undertake continuing professional development. Language competence and professional expertise can quickly erode or become out of date in a rapidly changing context. Interpreters and translators, like other colleagues in the public services, are expected to keep their skills honed (see Chapter 4). Regular re-registration arrangements should require evidence of activities for this purpose.

Levels of membership of the register

It is unlikely that sufficient numbers of interpreters or translators will be available immediately in all the language combinations required. Therefore, in order to accommodate the transitional period, while the register is being built up, different but defined levels of competence are likely to be adopted.

These may include full membership for those who have satisfied all the criteria; interim membership for those who, for example, have passed the relevant examinations but not yet had sufficient proven experience and a rare language category where only limited objective evidence of competence is available. One reason for this would be because there are currently no examinations available in one of the two languages involved. Those registered at interim level have specified timescales in which to upgrade, lest they be tempted to remain on the register without properly meeting the standards required for the task.

All those registered in whatever category would, however, be obliged to observe the code of conduct described in Chapter 3. This includes the requirement to admit to professional limitations. Knowing when you don't know is an essential prerequisite for any professional, and all the more vital when operating with limited skills. It could be argued that having people on the register with limited skills is counterproductive, but it does allow carefully selected candidates to progress upwards within specified timescales. It is essential that the clients are aware in advance to which level of registration an interpreter belongs.

Code of professional conduct/ethics

As mentioned above, every registered interpreter, at any level, should sign an agreement to observe the code of conduct. The code is the cornerstone of a profession, and promoting its implementation is one of the essential tasks of a professional body. A profession normally supports implementation of its code in four ways:

Training

As described in Chapter 4, strategies to promote understanding and application of the code, and the reasons underpinning each section of it, are integral to every stage of training – so that even when dealing with a road traffic accident at 3 a.m. on the hard shoulder of a motorway, the interpreter immediately knows how to proceed.

Example

Learning from experienced practitioners who have become adept not only at observing their code but also at resolving challenges that may obstruct its observance and ethical dilemmas. As solo practitioners, interpreters may not often work with colleagues, but it can be instructive when they do.

Interdisciplinary conventions

Colleagues in other professions will also be adhering to their own codes. All professional codes have much in common, such as confidentiality and impartiality, and are therefore mutually supportive. These colleagues should also be able to recognise and respect the aims of the interpreter's or translator's code if it is explained to them.

Disciplinary procedures

A code has to be enforceable if it is to be worth anything. The profession as a whole has to be able to take action if, for example, an interpreter commits a range of infringements from being constantly late or making minor repeated errors to the major infringements of deliberate misinterpreting, corruption or working under the influence of alcohol or drugs. The disciplinary process is an essential, if not often a happy, process and part of being responsible for one's own profession.

Complaints may come from a variety of sources, such as the public services, other-language speaking clients or other interpreters. Formally regulated professions do not normally discipline each other's members. Public service linguists would not take it upon themselves to take action if, for example, a doctor or a lawyer infringed their own professional codes. They would report the individual concerned to the relevant professional line manager or body for them to take action in respect of its own member where appropriate. The same can happen in reverse.

Disciplinary procedures may vary in detail from country to country, and for many, they are a work in progress. As an example of established disciplinary procedures, see the UK's National Register for Public Service Interpreters (www.nrpsi.co.uk) although that too may adapt to fit into any changes required by the broader professional and legislative context.

Several interesting points arise in relation to disciplinary procedures, which will have to be resolved with time and experience. They include the principles of the Human Rights legislation that is beginning to have a bearing on professional disciplinary procedures. Traditionally, members can be struck off a professional register, but should an individual potentially be deprived of their livelihood without the involvement of a full and public legal hearing? Or should outside people be brought in to share or carry out the adjudication[2].

Once public service interpreters begin to work in countries other than their own, which country's professional body is responsible should disciplinary proceedings be called for? Will an international approach emerge? It seems excessively bureaucratic to require interpreters to register in each country when they may only be working there for a day. Could there be an international register? Would this come gradually through professional language bodies in individual countries recognising the members of one and then two or more other countries? Or, is it easier to monitor our own national registers and seek equivalent standards of training and practice?

The relationships between a profession's disciplinary procedures, the contractual arrangements between any employer and members of a profession and the civil and criminal justice system will depend upon national conventions.

Employment structures

A professional register does not necessarily provide an immediate interface between interpreters and their clients. It is not necessary to contact a national medical council to gain access to the services of a doctor. One goes to a clinic or hospital where the doctors all belong to their medical register and abide by its standards.

In the absence of a clearly defined location such as a medical practice or law firm, structures to provide this daily interface are developing gradually, at different paces and according to different cultural conventions for public service interpreters and translators. Broadly speaking, there are three general approaches in the public service context. Sometimes all three may be operating in combination within a particular country.

One model is the full or part-time employment of interpreters in a public service locale, such as a hospital that has a large number of patients from one language group. This approach does not normally include the legal services: the title 'police interpreter', for example, does not support a perception of impartiality.

Interpreters and translators employed directly by a public service will have the usual contract of employment and, with that, a job description. It is likely that they will also be subject to the supervision, appraisal systems and benefits according to the employment law of the country concerned. These should not mean that they are not also subject to the standards and requirements of their profession in the same way as other professionals.

Inevitably, a public service cannot directly employ sufficient interpreters to cover all the language combinations they may need, and they will turn to the approaches below when necessary.

In the second approach, public services contact self-employed registered interpreters who undertake freelance work, and engage them on a sessional basis. Many freelance interpreters prefer not to be associated with an interpreting and translation agency, particularly where that means that they are paid less because of the administrative top slice taken by the agency out of the public service payment. This direct contact method is becoming rarer in countries where public service interpreting is more established and there is a greater demand. Public service personnel can find it time-consuming to locate interpreters in the right language combinations, even with access to an interpreters' professional register. It is the interpreter in these circumstances who can be particularly isolated and exposed unless there are structures to provide them with professional support such as mentoring and continuing professional development.

The third approach is for the interpreter to undertake self-employed sessional work through an interpreting and translation agency. These can be commercial or non-profit-making organisations, depending on national approaches. In the USA, for example, it seems that commercial competitive agencies are more usual, while Europe, Canada and Australia tend to favour the not-for-profit agency route that corresponds to the not-for-profit national health and other public services. Whichever type is used, they need to have proven suitable financial and administrative structures and systems; a national system for agency accreditation is worthy of consideration. The introduction of national recommended fee scales, to be applied whether or not an intermediary is involved, mitigates one of the main disadvantages of the use of agencies.

Commercial agencies are profit driven and therefore less of the money available may go to the interpreter. Many will be satisfactory and will seek to uphold standards and good employment practice. Some may not be, and can take a large percentage of the fee for themselves, may not properly check the qualifications of the interpreter or translator they employ and may not pay them in a timely manner.

The best not-for-profit local or regional agencies tend to be more rounded and invest in supportive activities. They may be funded through service-level agreements with local public services. That is, a public service will pass on its interpreting budget for the year and be invoiced per session accordingly. The administration percentage taken from the public service fees will all be reinvested in agency's activities. These organisations may either be providing expertise for one large organisation, such as a large hospital or metropolitan police force, or for all the public services in a locality.

The better agencies will operate a one-stop twenty-four hour contact system seven days a week for local public services and deal with all associated administration. As part of that, they will take requests for interpreting assistance on an informed basis, select the most appropriate registered interpreters for assignments, brief interpreters adequately and, where appropriate, de-brief interpreters after assignments and pay them within a set time.

Just as importantly, they will provide training, support, mentoring, supervision, continuing professional development and quality assurance according to emerging national standards. Many will also deal with translations. They will participate in training public service providers in how to work with interpreters and translators, liaise with the public services over problem-solving and with local other-language speaking groups.

These local or regional agencies provide the mechanisms and support for growth and development, are responsive to local needs, are cost-effective and monitor closely the quality of their work against national standards. In the countries where such not-for-profit agencies are developing, one can anticipate a situation where national standards for their administration could soon produce a nationally consistent level of quality assurance. This would enable those involved to agree upon such strategies as offering training not only to the language combinations most needed locally but also to cover, between them, the languages needed less often to ensure the widest possible national coverage of languages and language varieties.

Such arrangements also include the capability for interchanging interpreters where situations demand it. There are occasions when it could be insensitive or unsafe to employ a local interpreter, particularly where the language groups are small in number, for example, in a situation where there is a bitterly contested domestic dispute or where there has been violence as a result of political dispute. An organised national structure also makes it possible to call upon large numbers of qualified interpreters quickly, for example in an emergency, such as a plane or road accident.

There are other benefits to having such a structure, which include using nationally compatible software and other systems. Software should cover the whole range of languages including characters from French and German as well as different scripts such as Urdu and Chinese. There could also be a shared database of standard translated texts: it is neither cost-effective nor sensible to have the same form or the same instructions translated many times in 20 areas of a country.

Interpreters are often involved in running such agencies, either on a full-time basis or part-time along with continuing to practise as interpreters. Clearly they are often the best people to do that. Few people can support working interpreters better than another skilled interpreter. The necessary specific and general management skills required are emerging into a coherent form and being learnt.

Employment contracts or letters of agreement

The moment when an interpreter receives a telephone call to come to the aid of a foreign lorry driver trapped in his cab, or a woman in labour, is not the time to negotiate the details of engagement arrangements. These should already be in place, and are usually negotiated between an interpreter and a public service or between an agency (commercial or not-for-profit) and senior managers of the public services. They should be fully understood, and agreed in advance, by all the parties involved.

Claiming fees and expenses subsequently can be an uphill struggle for an interpreter if agreement templates are not in place.

Such agreements should include the following basic items:

- the date, time and location of the assignment
- estimated duration
- description of the assignment e.g. 54-year-old man with gastric ulcer visiting clinic for medical consultation
- language – and language variety where applicable
- any special features, for example, child abuse
- fees payable per hour, with any variations during out-of-office hours, night time and public holidays. Note that the same hourly fees will normally be charged for any time spent waiting, for example, in a court house until the case to be interpreted comes on
- travel time per hour if this is longer than an hour
- cancellation fees where an assignment has been booked but has not taken place, where loss of earnings from rejecting other assignments can be proved
- reasonable expenses in terms of car mileage, train and bus fares and car parking charges
- subsistence expenses in terms of food and, although more rarely needed, hotel accommodation
- practical mechanisms for paying fees and expenses, normally within 30 days
- insurance arrangements, both personal and professional indemnity
- tax implications, that is whether tax is deducted at source or has to be declared by the individual in an annual return to the tax office.

Interpreters, in their turn, also agree to observe their own code of ethics, any good practice guidelines agreed between the public sector and themselves and health and safety regulations.

Copies should be signed, and retained, by both the interpreter and the public service personnel. The specialist local agencies are likely to deal with these overall, so that the interpreter does not have to attend to them on each individual occasion. But the interpreter should make sure that they are in place.

It may be useful to say something more about insurance because it may not be needed often but, when it is, it is essential in the public service context where the risks to life and liberty may be greater than in other fields. Professional legal indemnity insurance applies to professional practice where, for example, an interpreter is sued in a case where the wrong limb was operated on. It may not be the interpreter's fault but a defence is needed. It is rare, however, that any insurance will protect a practitioner from negligence. Insurance against personal injury may be covered by the public service if, for example, the ambulance crashes, but being attacked by a violent or drunken client may not. Professional language bodies may offer cheaper insurance cover to their members, and employment agencies may cover their sessional employees. It is worth checking out such details carefully before undertaking any interpreting or translation assignments. Provision for such factors as sickness pay and pension contributions will depend upon national agreements.

Trade Unions

Professional bodies and their registers do not usually operate as trade unions. While they promote standards and good practice, they may not (and perhaps should not) be in the business of negotiating pay and working arrangements and fighting the corner of individuals where conflicts arise in these matters.

Many countries traditionally have trade unions whose role is to avoid and pre-empt any such conflict by skilful and ongoing diplomacy to produce the optimum balanced deal for their members. As a consequence their union members are reasonably paid and enjoy reasonable working conditions and the employer and/or clients are not exploited. The last situation may seem unlikely but it has been known for an interpreter, with a rare language combination, to raise their fees beyond what would normally be considered acceptable to a public service required by law to employ an interpreter where one is needed.

Trade Unions also have long experience and expertise in other areas such as health and safety matters. They are able to provide researched advice on, for example, how interpreters may protect themselves and be protected from infectious diseases such as AIDS. They can also act a source of advice on employment and legal matters.

In conclusion, the more structured approach of the public service context may at first seem unduly rigorous to the practitioner new to that field. In fact, it should provide a more secure and supportive framework within which to practise. It has been developed through years of experience and is still evolving and changing with experience. The newly qualified public service interpreter is trained to know the structure and to understand the principles that underpin it, so that they can contribute to its improvement over time.

Moreover, the public services themselves are gradually recognising the importance of having a professional framework for the interpreters and translators they work with. The front line practitioners, such as doctors and lawyers who are members of professions, appreciate the principles involved and the reasons for them, and are supportive of that development for public service linguists.

Protection of title is being considered in a number of countries such as the Netherlands. Protection of title would mean that only individuals who had met certain professional standards would be able to call themselves 'interpreters' or 'translators'. Just as no one can call themselves a 'doctor' or a 'lawyer' unless they have met specified criteria, so no one could call themselves an 'interpreter' or a 'translator' unless they met specified criteria. That could be a worthwhile long-term goal. But a good deal has to be put in place before that can happen in terms of establishing training and practice standards and in having a sufficient number of qualified interpreters and translators for it to be feasible.

Suggested activities

- Find out whether there are national professional language bodies and registers in your own country. If so, what are their codes of conduct and disciplinary procedures?
- What criteria could be used in a system to accredit public service interpreting and translation agencies?
- What recourse do you have if you are not paid for an assignment and what are the best ways of protecting yourself from being in that position?

Further reading

Corsellis, A. (2000) 'Turning Good Intentions into Good Practice. Enabling the Public Services to Fulfil their Responsibilities', in R. Roberts, S. Carr, D. Abraham and A. Dufour (eds) *The Critical Link 2: Interpreters in the Community* (pp. 89–100). Amsterdam: John Benjamins.

Corsellis, A. (2003) 'Interpreting and Translation in the UK Public Services: The Pursuit of Excellence versus, and via, Expediency', in M. Rogers and G. Anderman (eds) *Translation Today: Trends and Perspectives* (pp.180–91). Clevedon: Multilingual Matters.

Corsellis, A., Hertog, E., Martinsen, B., Ostarhild, E. and Vanden Bosch, Y. (2003) 'European Equivalencies in Legal Interpreting and Translation', in L. Brunette, G. Bastian, I., Hemlin and H. Clarke (eds) *The Critical Link 3. Interpreters in the Community* (pp. 293–305). Amsterdam: John Benjamins.

Hale, S. (2007) *Community Interpreting*. Palgrave Macmillan.

Lascar, E. (1997) 'Accreditation in Australia. An alternative means' in A. Carr, R. Roberts, A. Dufour and D. Steyn (eds) *The Critical Link 1. Interpreters in the Community* (109–18). Amsterdam: John Benjamins.

Roberts, R. (2002) 'Community Interpreting: A Profession in Search of Its Identity', in E. Hung (ed.) *Teaching Translation and Interpreting 4 Building Bridges* (157–75). Amsterdam: John Benjamins.

Website

http://www.cps.gov.uk/publications/agencies/interpret.html (Trials Issues Group Revised Agreement on The Arrangements for The Attendance of Interpreters in Investigations and Proceedings within The Criminal Justice System).

6
Bilingual Practitioners

This chapter tackles the range of factors which distinguish what are known as 'bilingual practitioners' working in the public services from public service interpreters and translators. The term 'bilingual' is used here simply because it is a commonly used term to denote those who have a working command of two languages, although the term can indicate varying degrees of functionality between the two languages, with the fully balanced bilingual being the exception rather than the rule (Baker 2000: 82). The term 'practitioner' is used to cover the whole range of professional and vocational employees of the public services, from school dinner supervisors to senior medical consultants.

'Bilingual practitioner' is therefore a short title to refer to individuals who are qualified to deliver their particular expertise in two languages. They are increasingly valued as part of the means of provision of service to a multilingual constituency, and dual qualifications should be encouraged as speech communities become stabilised.

The need for bilingual practitioners

The invaluable potential of having a multilingual and multicultural workforce has rarely been properly thought through and developed. The full potential of a valuable resource is therefore often lost.

Suitably qualified employees with bilingual language skills can operate in a range of functions and at a range of levels. For example, in local areas with a preponderance of specific languages, at a basic level bilingual receptionists can provide a welcome to other-language speakers at the front office, take and make telephone calls involving routine messages and set individuals on their way through appointments and processes in a language familiar to them. Bilingual school dinner assistants and playground supervisors have a similarly useful role. At a more specialised level, bilingual practitioners may include trained medical staff.

Indeed, bilingual practitioners are particularly useful at higher professional levels in circumstances where working through an interpreter is impractical or challenging. It would not be impossible to work through an interpreter in such cases, and many interpreters do so on a daily basis with some sensitivity, but it might be easier and more effective not to have to.

These circumstances include three broad areas. The first is where the interpreting process itself may be difficult for the client, including, for instance, the very young or the elderly. Children can find the interpreting process bewildering and there are occasions such as cases of alleged child abuse where the information exchange is fragile enough as it is without adding complications. For the elderly, in cases where there is an element of mental confusion, there is comfort and clarity in communicating directly in one's own language.

The second circumstance includes such events as diagnostic psychiatry, where the clinical symptoms of a disorder may be embedded in how patients express themselves. A non-medically qualified interpreter is unlikely to recognise their entire significance or be able to transfer the message completely with all those vital diagnostic clues intact. Equally, the psychiatrist without a true understanding of a patient's particular culture would be hampered in recognising the symptoms if they were transferred in such circumstances. The phrases and concepts used to characterise depression, for example, differ between cultures.

In diagnostic speech therapy (Baker 2006), particularly in relation to children brought up in a bilingual environment, a bilingual speech therapist may be the best equipped to assess a child's speech development and to suggest remedies if necessary. The situation of an elderly victim of a stroke that has affected his or her speech may be more easily assessed by a speech therapist who can speak the language concerned. The same applies in cases where probation officers are required to assess offenders' cognitive development to ascertain the suitability of programmes which might successfully confront offending behaviour. All these are difficult enough tasks when conducted through a shared language and culture, and outcomes are likely to be diminished if the consultation crosses languages and cultures.

The third and related circumstance is where the interpreting process could impede subtle interchanges which are part of the provision of a service, such as counselling or therapy. It is not just the meaning of the messages to be exchanged but the cultural conventions of such aspects as turn taking and the necessary relationship with the counsellor (as opposed to the interpreter) that is relevant. Therapeutic relationships and the way conversations are conducted between patients and their 'healers' may differ between cultures and between individuals within those cultures.

Likely existing arrangements

It will be clear from the various situations described above that the role of the bilingual practitioner is a responsible one at any level. Yet, like the skills required for interpreting, the set of skills required for bilingual practitioners has too often been underestimated. It has been assumed, for example, that simply because a member of staff has another cultural background or claims to have a degree of competence in another language, they can satisfactorily accomplish any task in the other language even if it is beyond their level of professional and linguistic competence. There have been reported instances of public authorities employing people simply on the basis of their ethnic origin, and without the necessary proven skills, just to present a cosmetic image of diversity in their workplace. Such approaches are unfair to all concerned.

Many bilingual employees refuse to be so used or try to avoid being put in that position. They are acutely aware that, for example, possessing a limited domestic command of a language does not equip one to explain the technicalities of an operation consent form or to shoulder the legal consequences. A shaky grasp of holiday Spanish will not enable an English lawyer to take instructions from a Spanish-speaking client. They know their own jobs well enough to appreciate that being asked, simply on the basis of unproven language competence, to carry out a task beyond their professional training and level of skill is fraught with risk. First-year mental health nursing student should not be asked to deal with violent schizophrenics simply on the basis that she or he shares a language with them.

In addition, having fought to gain qualifications, many know from experience that their career development can be jeopardised if they become too useful for dealing with one particular aspect of their professional work that involves other-language speakers. Young bilingual doctors may be glad to do their turn in the antenatal clinics with patients with whom they share a language but may also wish to have the opportunity to train as neurosurgeons.

Many others have been pressured into providing assistance in the interests of humanity and on the basis of spurious assumptions about shared ethnic origin but against their better professional judgement.

In some countries, however, especially those that are traditionally multilingual, untold numbers of public service providers will see using their second and third language skills as simply part of their job. In South Africa, for example, there are eleven official languages, which include English and Afrikaans as well as indigenous African languages. Nurses in parts of that country have traditionally acted as language bridges between patients and doctors, although it is said that difficulties have arisen with the recent arrival of Spanish-speaking Cuban doctors because Spanish is not one of the languages usually spoken by staff.

Overall, there is a real need to regularise arrangements for the bilingual employee in order to protect them, to protect their clients and to protect their service. In addition, there is a need to maximise the resource, to define the level of skills needed, to provide training and assessment and to deploy and employ the people who hold relevant qualifications appropriately.

Target skills

The bilingual practitioner clearly needs two sets of proven skills: language skills to communicate with their professional colleagues and with their other-language speaking clients, as well as the professional or vocational skills to deliver their expertise safely and effectively in two cultures. Both need to be at the level, and of the type, necessary for the task in hand.

Bilingual receptionists, for example, need to have a minimum of school-leaving level written and spoken skills in both languages with training in the communication strategies and vocabulary necessary to welcome people appropriately, use the telephone and to read and write simple messages accurately. They also need the skills of a receptionist in knowing how to make appropriate records (probably using a computer), using the correct naming systems, who to contact when, and how to manage a waiting area.

Similarly, bilingual nursery nurses need to have a sound written and spoken competence in both languages to communicate with both new arrivals and their children. They need to be able not only to support the children through the start of their own bilingual journey but also to understand sufficiently the child's needs and feelings. When parents bring and collect the children, accurate information needs to be exchanged on such vital matters as aspects of physical health, the child's physical, emotional and social development (sharing and collaborating on such matters as recognising colours, numbers and constructive play) and anything happening at home that might affect the child's behaviour in nursery. The good nursery has become of particular importance to young parents who are new arrivals and may not have their own parents available to give them advice and much needed support while they are obliged to work long hours to establish themselves. The modest investment in the training and employment of qualified bilingual nursery nurses has profound potential benefits for the next generation.

To take examples from another professional category, the bilingual psychiatrist, speech therapist or counsellor will need postgraduate level skills in both languages, an adequate understanding of both the cultures underpinning those languages as well as the professional skills and competence required to deliver their expertise.

Likely existing skills

Despite the amount and range of language skills possessed by numerous individuals, their bilingualism is usually incomplete and inadequate for the purpose of working as a bilingual practitioner. Spoken or written language skills may be much weaker in one or the other language. Terminology may be limited to the context in which it has been used – well illustrated by the respected teacher of Italian who realised that he did not have the Italian vocabulary associated with mortgages because he had left Italy when he was nineteen, and had had no occasion then or since to negotiate a mortgage in Italian. Registers may be limited to, for example, the formal academic or the domestic. A wide and objective appreciation of the culture bases underpinning the languages may not be sufficiently developed. Nonetheless, the necessary potential exists for development. The numbers of such individuals with these potential skills increase with the global movement of people.

Those who have the potential to become bilingual practitioners comprise two broad groups. The first have an existing good command of the language of the country or region concerned. Many immigrants are particularly ambitious for their children to advance professionally. Others may be new arrivals but have existing solid second language skills, although they are likely to be confined to limited registers.

Those who have been brought up in the area of the majority language but come from other-language speaking homes and backgrounds are likely to have a full command of the majority language for both professional and social purposes but a mainly domestic command of their other language. They will have used that language at home, to chat informally with relatives and perhaps for religious purposes but rarely extend that to the vocabulary and conventions of communication in professional life. In addition, the language used in diasporic speech communities tends not to develop in the same way as that in the original speech community (see, for instance, Mühleisen's study of Caribbean English-based Creole, Mühleisen 2002).

The second group comprise individuals doing relatively low-level jobs which do not demand high-level competence in the majority or official language, even though they may be qualified to do more senior work in their country of origin. As their second language competence increases, members of this group are likely to be available for other training and posts. Those who have qualified, for example, as doctors and nurses abroad, will be fully fluent and literate in their first language. In some cases, particularly where English is concerned, at least part of their education may have been conducted in their second language. Many in the UK, for example, have been used to reading professional journals and communicating with colleagues in English. What that does not equip them to do, however, is to communicate with patients or other clients who speak local dialects and use euphemisms.

In both categories there is likely to be a need to develop a greater understanding of one or other culture base in relation to their languages. There is also a need to bear in mind the range of cultural backgrounds of individuals and language varieties: Spanish speakers may come from South or Central America as well as from Spain, French speakers from Africa as well as France and Gujarati speakers may come from Gujarat or East Africa.

Selection, training and assessment

Formal combined language and professional/vocational training already exists in some countries and for some purposes. There are established language and business degrees, for example. In respect of the public service sector, combined law and language degrees are well known. Police officers in some countries such as Belgium and the Netherlands are required to take language tests. Some universities on the Indian subcontinent require study in an additional language as part of any degree course. What follows are simple suggestions as to how to take this approach forward on a broader scale.

It must be accepted that working as a bilingual practitioner is a matter of choice, unless it is part of the recognised job description. Not every bilingual wishes to work in a bilingual capacity. Their interests and talents may lie elsewhere or they may be reluctant to do so as a

result of an unfortunate past experience. It may take time for worthwhile arrangements to be developed, established and recognised. Then
it should be possible for people to move in and out of working as bilingual practitioners, according to their professional and personal circumstances and wishes.

The first criterion for selection for training should be a positive interest in working in the bilingual context and a sensible appreciation of
what that may involve. Other criteria include assessments at the appropriate level of all four skills in both languages (reading, writing, speaking
and listening) and evidence of an understanding of the underpinning
cultures. Clearly, there have to be relevant professional or vocational
qualifications in, for example, psychiatry or speech therapy, and above-
average interpersonal and problem-solving skills.

Interviews may be carried out to determine aptitude and structured
references taken up. The process of assessment should be conducted
by senior bilingual professionals, where these exist. Where they do not
yet exist, selection tasks could be assessed by experts in the relevant
fields such as language and law or medicine or nursery nursing.
Information should be given as well as received, so that candidates are
clear about what is involved in training, assessments, future work and
career prospects.

The length of any course depends upon the level and type of existing
skills measured against the targets. Individual students can be recommended to enhance one aspect of their existing skills, e.g. one language,
before starting training. The course format can be organised according
to circumstances and can be full-time or part-time.

The training of those selected should include the following components at the appropriate levels. Language enhancement, to cover all the
formal and informal terminology likely to be involved in professional
or vocational work, is one essential element. That includes exploration
of the relationships between the terms that express the same, or similar,
concepts in both languages. As a result, differences are also revealed
about procedures and processes; the English term 'bail', for example,
can have a linguistic equivalent in the other language, but the actual
legal significance may differ and procedures may be implemented differently in other jurisdictions. As with interpreters, informal language,
including the range of euphemisms, slang used by the young and jargon used within the public services, is also required.

The cultural underpinning to both verbal communication and the
provision of expertise has to be explored and understood. As each individual client will have a unique background arising from his or her own

life experience, the principles for bilingual practice should be identified for the practitioner to adapt to individual circumstances against a sound background understanding of the cultures of both working languages. Even working within one culture, public service practitioners already adapt their expertise to individuals. They can accommodate what they do for the young and the old, the well educated and the illiterate, the serene and the distressed and those who can cope with kidney dialysis at home and those who cannot. Working into a second culture is fundamentally about extending those skills.

Courses benefit from contributions from other disciplines with relevant insights. Medical anthropologists, for example, study different cultural approaches to health and healing. Social anthropologists study a useful range of aspects, such as different views of natural justice and family dynamics. These contributions from academics promote the concept of objective approaches to differences between cultures, without necessarily attaching value judgements or stereotyping. They also allow participants to think through potential problems concerning the varying degrees of acceptability in different cultures of, for instance, practices such as domestic violence or female circumcision. Negotiating the family dynamics in one culture against the institutional dynamics of the public service is likely to be another challenge. In matriarchal societies, some grandmothers could insist on taking a leading part in decision-making within their extended families, while the public services in other societies require decision-making to be limited to the particular family members involved. The concept of confidentiality also differs between cultures and groups. Sensitive work that respects each individual's starting points has to be done with all parties to preserve the integrity of the family dynamic.

Training for work in particular fields requires an understanding of what is needed to accommodate a second group of cultural backgrounds while recognising how much is held in common. Psychiatrists need to appreciate how different mental health conditions may be expressed and perceived in order to be able to treat them. The story is told, for example, of the male patient who was recovering from a mental illness and knelt down at the feet of the English psychiatrist. It had to be explained to the alarmed English doctor that this did not mean that his patient had relapsed but was respectfully greeting him as a father.

Nursery nurses need an appreciation of potential different approaches and attitudes to child rearing. The many aspects of weaning, food, toilet training, play and discipline require ongoing conversations if the required collaborations between parents and nurses are to be reached.

A deeper understanding of the relationships between languages and cultures promotes not only the functioning of the bilingual practitioner but also of their own bilingual, bicultural personalities and make-up, in the same way as it does for interpreters and translators. It has to be recognised that sometimes that process can be a bit uncomfortable. Some may have found it difficult in their teenage years to reconcile the various parts of their backgrounds and welcome the opportunity to explore them for themselves and for their own children. The sum of those parts in comfortable co-existence is likely to add up to something richer than the separate components. There is, as with training interpreters, often an identifiable moment when things fall into place and the students move forward with confidence to gain huge enjoyment in extending their bilingualism and biculturalism.

Objective assessment of the range of skills is necessary before successful candidates are allowed to practise as qualified bilingual practitioners. Assessment methods can vary according to the discipline involved so long as standards to match the task are not compromised. These may include a combination of written formal papers, project work, portfolios and on-the-job assessments. The assessors should obviously themselves possess the right standard and range of skills to enable them to make an informed judgement according to defined criteria as set out in validated course documentation. National, or even international, recognition of qualifications has clear benefits. Integral to the training are the aspects of practice set out in the next section.

Planning and organisation of work

As pointed out in Chapter 1, there are some 300 languages spoken in London. Other large cities may have similar language demographics. In more rural areas, there are likely to be small groups of other-language speakers whose needs may be greater because of their isolation. There are therefore clear logistical challenges to matching the supply of bilingual practitioners to where they are most needed. Successful examples of intelligent and imaginative good practice can promote dissemination and development.

Bilingual practitioners may, especially at the outset, have to work carefully with others to plan how their work should be organised to ensure that their skills are deployed appropriately and sufficiently, and to avoid too much being demanded of them in the workplace.

First of all, it is important that colleagues and line managers appreciate fully the role and level of expertise of the bilingual practitioner. Those skills should then be deployed where they best meet client requirements. This may involve a straightforward work placement in, for example, a nursery or speech therapy unit, where there is a significant number of other-language speakers to warrant the employment of a full or part-time bilingual practitioner. Alternatively, the bilingual practitioner may be more peripatetic and work over a geographical area dealing with other-language speakers who may, for example, attend different clinics on an ad hoc or group basis. This last approach requires good practical organisational skills similar to those needed by Public Service Interpreters (PSIs) (see Chapter 3).

Bilingual practitioners should not normally be used as interpreters or translators. Firstly, without the necessary training, they may not possess the relevant transfer skills. Secondly, their time is best used for their primary role.

Mention must also be made of the practitioner taking their share of responsibility for setting out contracts and job descriptions that reflect their skills adequately and appropriately. While these are primarily the responsibility of management, there is little benefit to be gained from signing a document and then complaining about it afterwards. It may take time, however, for additional language and professional cultural skills to attract the additional salaries they deserve in parts of the public sector.

Accountability, lines of communication and record keeping

The arrangements for these aspects of work have to be negotiated and set out with absolute clarity. Bilingual practitioners can feel almost detached from the main body of the particular public service while they immerse themselves in another language and culture. They are not, and remain an integral part of the service.

The very fact that they are working in another language and culture to which other colleagues may not have access requires them to pay close attention to keeping senior colleagues, to whom they are accountable, fully informed and who are responsible for them and their work. At a basic level, the bilingual nursery nurse must take care to report to his or her supervisor with information about incidents or home developments concerning particular children. The bilingual psychiatrist or nurse must report to colleagues when a patient displays suicidal or violent tendencies. Senior probation officers, doctors, nurses, police officers, local government officials and the like have the right to know exactly what is happening on their watch.

Equally, other colleagues need to be kept informed so that they can properly carry out their responsibilities, especially because the bilingual colleague may not be always present. Information should never be held by only one person. Other nursery nurses can give special attention to the child in question. Other health care staff can look out for the suicidal patient. Actions and developments can be reported back.

Careful record keeping, in a format agreed by the particular public service, is an integral part of the process. The usual differentiations are made between facts and opinions. Risk assessments should be noted. Record keeping enables appropriate colleagues to be kept informed and promotes best practice. It promotes the integration of other-language speakers within the mainstream of the service and discourages any thought that this work might be peripheral or second-class in any way. It has to be said that record keeping also provides a measure of protection to the bilingual practitioners for, in the same way that there are those who will always blame the interpreter when matters go awry, the same can happen to the bilingual practitioner.

Where the other-language speaking clients move between departments, care should be taken to record relevant additional objective information to enable colleagues, including other bilingual practitioners, to understand the situation of the individual better. Simple matters such as food preferences can make a worthwhile difference to quality of service. Significant cultural or cross-cultural information and explanations relating to such matters as medical diagnoses and treatment, alleged criminal behaviour or family dynamics allow colleagues access to a greater depth of information to inform their own approaches.

Informed supervision, mentoring and monitoring

One of the reasons why bilingual practice can make both practitioners and managers nervous is the absence of adequate strategies for supervising, mentoring and monitoring within the existing institutional frameworks which do not take sufficient account of the bilingual practitioner. The normal checks and balances to ensure good practice are therefore not always operable as colleagues who do not share the other language may be excluded from discussions, interviews or consultations. Bilingual practitioners can therefore feel unsupported and their colleagues can feel that they do not know what is happening and have no control over activities conducted through the medium of the other language. These are reasonable and proper concerns, but it is possible to develop the necessary strategies with the mature co-operation of the bilingual practitioner.

Inevitably, there can be a time lag before sufficient qualified and experienced bilingual practitioners are in place to supervise and support more junior colleagues against clear and transparent guidelines. Meanwhile, a collaborative multidisciplinary approach can be taken whereby interpreters and translators take care of the language side and those with expertise in the professional/vocational aspects supervise and support (take care of) those. This hybrid and hopefully interim arrangement has its advantages because it educates colleagues. The senior health care worker, social worker or local authority official has to give serious thought to the implications involved, about how quality can be monitored, how regular appraisals might be conducted and how challenges and problems can be dealt with on a day-to-day basis.

Some strategies are emerging. In certain countries, for example, bilingual police officers are not allowed to participate as part of the investigative team beyond a particular point. In other services, anecdotal reports suggest that recognition is being given to the worthwhile contributions bilingual practitioners can make to improve the service for their particular language speakers. These, in turn, often improve the service for all by offering a greater variety of options.

Continuing professional and personal development

Successful practitioners need formal and informal structures through which they can develop and improve on what they do on a daily basis. The bilingual practitioner should have full access to the regular strategies for continuing professional development (CPD) such as the seminars, in-service training and conferences that are a normal part of professional life in many countries.

What they may not have full access to is continuing professional development for the additional language and the cultural aspects of their expertise. In time, CPD is likely to become more structured as the role of the bilingual practitioner becomes established. One can envisage the emergence of national and international gatherings, information resources and literature for specific activities. Meanwhile, it may be considered useful to start formalising this process through the interdisciplinary supervision and mentoring arrangements set out above.

Career progression and training in new areas should not be overlooked: promotion is usually determined by criteria which relate to *professional* expertise, which may need to be developed outside bilingual activities. And bilingual colleagues who prove invaluable to the smooth and efficient operation of a professional unit or team may not be willingly released from their bilingual work by their managers or senior colleagues in order to undertake further training or to broaden their professional experience. There are benefits which accrue from senior members of any profession or vocation gathering experience as bilingual practitioners, as insights gained can be applied to their work at policy and decision-making levels.

Personal development is an integral part of continuing professional development activity. Being a bilingual practitioner can be isolating, one can never share the full range of concerns and daily experiences with colleagues if they have not also experienced them. There are inevitable degrees of intercultural tensions, and working perpetually at the confluence of culture requires the strength of character and professionalism that has to grow with the experience. That enables the individual to absorb and analyse what happens in order to improve what they do next time, rather than to harden their reactions and deflect the necessary emotional journey.

So the bilingual practitioner should have access to whatever is needed to support and maintain his or her own personal development and to facilitate constructive reflection on experiences and reactions to them.

Codes of conduct or ethics

By definition, the bilingual practitioner is already a member of a profession or vocation and therefore bound by the associated codes of conduct. These are likely to include the standard core elements of such codes, such as requirements to:

- observe confidentiality
- act impartially
- practise to the best of one's ability and according to best practice
- admit professional limitations where necessary. This could include not interpreting or translating
- not bring the profession into disrepute
- support colleagues
- declare any conflicts of interest
- maintain and improve standards of personal professional or vocational skills.

These same elements of the code must also apply to the other half of the bilingual practitioner's expertise, linguistic/cultural skills and practice. If there are allegations of a breach of the code in terms of the professional/

vocational side, there are usually well-established methods of investigating and applying any disciplinary procedures. For example, if a doctor is alleged to have misbehaved, that may be dealt with by both the hospital that employs him and his professional medical body.

Matters are less well established in this regard for the bilingual practitioner and still need some careful thought. While medical negligence, for example, can potentially be dealt with through the medical profession's normal procedures, the situation for a bilingual practitioner can be more complex. For example, whoever investigates alleged linguistic incompetence would require adequate expertise in both bilingual and bicultural practice. Should alleged breaches in relation to language usage be investigated and dealt with by the relevant language professional body in cases where the practitioner is a member of it? That is a question still under debate, but the principles and process should be given careful consideration prior to their being needed.

Guidelines to good practice

As described in Chapter 3, while the codes of conduct or ethics encapsulate core principles, guidelines to good practice evolve in the light of experience as the best way of doing things and supporting the code. There are usually general guidelines and then a subset of guidelines for particular purposes. Guidelines are usually updated and disseminated nationally by the discipline concerned on a regular basis to ensure consistency and quality of service. They form a central element in training, so that students understand their purpose and how to follow them. They also learn the underlying principles so that, where practicalities preclude the following of the guidelines, alternative approaches can be responsibly identified and taken. For example, if the guidelines say that best practice requires that female bilingual nurses are to attend in the labour ward but the mother is haemorrhaging, that is no time to fuss about gender preferences.

Concrete examples of general guidelines for bilingual practitioners are hard to find but could usefully include the following:

- Before the assignment, bilingual practitioners should prepare themselves by clarifying the nature of the task, the linguistic and cultural background of the patient or other client and any other relevant further information to be gained from records and associated sources. This allows them to check that they have a language match and to make a judgement as to whether the task is within their competence.

They can also gather relevant materials that may be useful, such as information leaflets in that language and any resources needed to facilitate the likely outcomes of the task.

- During the assignment, the bilingual practitioner is likely to have to give more information to clients who are not familiar with the systems of the country. A bilingual lawyer, for instance, may have to provide wider explanations than normally if acting for an other-language client about to go to court for a drink-driving offence and will need to cover the status of the particular court, the role of the different people involved in the hearing, the procedures that will be followed and the practical significance of the likely outcomes. At the same time, the lawyer will gather more information than he or she might normally do in order to ascertain the client's perceptions of the event, attitudes and circumstances. Different jurisdictions vary in their approach to driving while drunk and, while ignorance of the law may be no defence, there may be mitigating factors. A senior London probation officer noted that driving without a licence in England could well seem a minor matter to a man who had been dodging bullets in a war zone two weeks earlier. As the interview draws to a close, the lawyer has to be as sure as possible that the most important information has been mutually understood. The client should know which court to go to, on what date and time and how to reach it and where in the building the lawyer will meet him. A map is always useful and mobile phone numbers should be exchanged in case of emergencies.
- After the assignment, arrangements will have to be made to enable the next step in any process. In the case of the drink-driver, for example, the lawyer may be the one who has to make arrangements to inform the court – if the police have not already done so – that the client does not speak the language of the court and to inform them which is the client's best language, so that the court staff can appoint an interpreter for the hearing and organise the court list to allow for extra time for the interpreted hearing.
- Records of each procedure will have to be kept, in line with the requirements of the public service, plus any additional information pertinent to the individual, which would be helpful to colleagues.
- Interpreters nearly always have their personal glossaries nearby and quickly take the opportunity to note down new or useful terminology in either language after assignments. The lawyer may have learnt some new terms relating to parts of a car or the latest slang about drinking, but is unlikely to need professional or personal support in

such a straightforward case. However, the male bilingual nurse who attends the haemorrhaging mother on an emergency basis, may need both professional and personal support, whatever the outcomes.

Conclusion: collaboration with interpreters and translators

Interpreters, translators and bilingual practitioners have different, defined roles but share much in common. In a working world where they are often relatively isolated, they are in a position to give each other mutual professional support over such matters as terminology and procedures.

There may be a number of occasions when people with all three skills sets are working on the same matter. Their combined professional expertise, where appropriate, could bring added value to their tasks. They can certainly add to each other's continuing professional development sessions where, for example, a bilingual lawyer can discuss changes in legislation or legal procedures and then discuss the linguistic implications with interpreter and translator colleagues. The three sets of language skills offer newly qualified linguists interesting options to choose from and a range of potential career moves for practitioners.

Further activities

- consider which public service procedures would best be dealt with by a bilingual practitioner, rather than an interpreter
- plan an outline course design for qualified psychotherapists, with some language skills, wishing to work through both languages.

Further reading

See www.cilt.org.uk for links to general language standards and European framework.

7
Responsibilities and Training of Public Service Staff

The story is told of a public service middle manager who was organising the recruitment of translators for a number of language combinations. When asked how he was going to select them, he replied that he had a very easy method. He would give each applicant for the job a text in English to translate. The applicants who achieved the same number of words as the source text in their translation into their target language would get the job. Now, the story may be apocryphal, but it reflects all too well, particularly in the English-speaking world, a general lack of understanding about languages and the work of translators and their colleagues, including those working in the public services.

When interpreters and translators are gathered together, lack of linguistic awareness among their clients is a frequently discussed subject. There is the low murmur of dissatisfaction as they share tales of unreasonable deadlines, the absence of briefing prior to assignments interpreting speeches on technical subjects and of speakers who mutter incoherently. The principal root of the concern is that an ill-informed client can affect the quality of the translator's or interpreter's work and therefore the outcomes of the event.

In the settings of international conferences, conventions have been established to overcome many of these hurdles, mainly thanks to the efforts of AIIC (the Association of International Conference Interpreters). Such conventions require, for example, that texts of speeches are provided for interpreters in advance to allow them to research and prepare terminology, and that translators have access to subject specialists. In commercial contexts, matters may be more problematic. Nevertheless, translators and interpreters operating in a business context usually manage to accommodate the linguistic shortcomings of their clients because the parties involved are more likely to be speaking the standard variety of their language and have a shared background understanding of the subject in hand, such as when two firms in the same line of business are negotiating an international contract about making washing machines.

Interpreters and translators who work in the contexts of international conferences or commerce would normally not consider they had a role to play in actually *training* their clients in how they might best work with them. Public service interpreters, however, can and do participate in such training in order to promote the optimum framework for them to carry out their own tasks to the highest possible standards, and to support their colleagues in other disciplines, such as medicine and law, in reaching their own standards of best practice. In the public service context, clients may speak a number of varieties of a language, not know much about one another, have an unequal understanding of the subject matter and each one may have much to lose. Given also that the interpreter may not have any time to prepare for the assignment, the possibilities of miscommunication rise proportionally in situations where accuracy is vital. Therefore the other professional disciplines should be in a position to share the responsibilities for the interlingual and intercultural nature of communication, and to provide a service to those with whom they do not share a language or culture.

This chapter discusses how that might be achieved. In some countries, including Canada, Australia, USA, Sweden and the UK, development work has been carried out to identify parallel skills for public service employees to complement those of interpreters and translators. These are by no means yet always implemented nationally and consistently but a useful start has been made. Evaluation of the outcomes has yet to be conducted on any scale. However, where these skills have been implemented by public services, interpreters and translators report a significant difference in improvement of their professional context and ability to do their own job. Public service employees also report a similar increase in improvement in their own abilities to work with linguists and across cultures. That brings with it an increase in job satisfaction, from doing tasks on the basis of an informed understanding and, in the process, seeing the subject less as a 'problem' and more as an interesting professional challenge. While there will clearly be national differences of approach, there is an emerging common ground. What follows is therefore a broad summary of what has been found to work in practice.

Why is training needed?

In many countries, there are overall existing legal, ethical and professional requirements for the public services to treat every individual equally, irrespective of language and culture. The implications are that each public service is responsible for finding out about the client(s), for example, their linguistic, cultural, social and economic background and their needs and perceptions; adapting their service, so far as possible, to their clients; informing their clients about their service; negotiating and delivering the best possible service; following quality assurance procedures and conducting research and development to improve their service. Communication with people who speak languages other than their own is necessary for each element listed.

It is not the interpreters' responsibility to absorb the whole impact of the interlingual, intercultural exchange. Nor could they do so and also carry out their own duties to the required standard. Indeed, interpreters are often not the best qualified to carry out these additional responsibilities. Therefore, colleagues in the public service disciplines have to be equipped to take on their share of the task effectively. An apparently straightforward opening exchange in a hearing in an English magistrates' court illustrates the point:

THE CLERK TO THE COURT:	Are you (name)?
DEFENDANT:	Yes
CLERK:	Where do you live?
DEFENDANT:	30 Maple Grove
CLERK:	What is your date of birth?
DEFENDANT:	11th October 1954
CLERK:	You are charged that on 2nd July 2004 you stole 3 DVDs from a shop belonging to HMV stores. Do you understand?
DEFENDANT:	Yes
CLERK:	I have to tell you that you may if you wish indicate a plea of guilty. If you do, the court will proceed on that basis. If you plead not guilty or give no plea at all then the court will hear representations about where the case should be tried and you may have a choice. I have to tell you that if you do indicate a plea of guilty and the Magistrates hear

	the facts, if when they have heard those facts they feel their powers of punishment are insufficient they may send you to the Judge at the Crown Court who has greater powers of punishment. Do you understand?
DEFENDANT:	Yes
CLERK:	Do you plead guilty or not guilty?
DEFENDANT:	Guilty
CLERK:	Please sit down while the facts are given to the court.

This imagined short exchange with fictitious date of birth, address, charge and other responses is a typical example of communication where there may be a lack of shared understanding of the context, procedures and terminology as well as the underlying principles involved. This does not only occur in the legal system. Being anxious may also hinder comprehension. Many of us leave doctors' surgeries without a precise idea of what has happened or what explanations have been given. Social workers have often developed an elliptical and indirect code of communication that may be deliberately non-specific, using vague words like 'issues' and phrases such as 'thank you for sharing that with me' (which may mean they do not agree with the speaker), 'you may care to reflect on that' (which may mean the speaker should agree) and, most testing of all to transfer, 'how do you feel about that?' (which could refer to a range of emotional, intellectual or physical reactions).

Public services have each developed and honed communication strategies, conventions and procedures to cover what needs to be done safely, efficiently and in the time allotted. In these circumstances, the interpreter cannot easily be responsible for all the dimensions necessary for accurate interlingual and intercultural exchange, as well as interpreting. As it is logistically impracticable to train members of the public who may potentially have dealings with the public services, it is helpful to train those working in the public services to work with interpreters and translators and across cultures and to be accountable for those skills.

To introduce the subject of divisions of responsibilities between the interpreter and the public service staff, it may be useful to pick up on some of the elements in the exchange from the magistrates' court above:

1. 'What is your name?' Awareness of when it is inappropriate to refer to 'Christian' names instead of 'first name' is now much higher in,

for instance, European countries. There is, however, much more to be considered. The clerk and records office should be well informed about the naming systems used in different cultures. In some, family names are placed in the middle and not at the end.

> Traditionally, the Chinese naming system consisted of a last name/ family name followed by personal name(s). Most personal names are gender specific. The importance of the family name is stressed by its being placed first in the sequence. Many British Chinese have adapted their names to follow the ethnic UK system. In addition to using their traditional Chinese names, many Chinese nowadays may also use a European personal name.
>
> Main components: personal name(s) + last name/family name
>
> Examples: Lan-Ying Cheung; Alison Wing; Wen-Zhi Man.
>
> (extract from *Naming Systems*, a training document published by the Judicial Studies Board in London 2005)

In other cultures, for example some Spanish speaking countries, a married woman keeps her maiden name combined with that of her husband's surname, and generations of the same family may not share the same last name. Rather confusingly, some other-language speakers will, in an effort to be helpful, change their names in ways that fit more easily into the conventions of the countries where they are living so that, for example, 'Wenpin' becomes 'Will' or 'Federico' becomes 'Fred'. Names have to be recorded precisely and consistently if individuals are not going to be wrongly arrested or, worse still, given the medical prescription or operation intended for someone else.

2. 'What is your date of birth?' The clerk should be aware that some people, particularly the elderly, may not know their date of birth if they come from countries or cultures where this fact was not of significance and records were not kept. Equally, although most countries now use the same method for official records, different traditional calendars exist, for example, such as the Chinese cyclical calendar.

3. 'You are charged that . . . ' Most court lawyers have perfected the art of re-coding the official wording to take account of native speakers who may not find that register easily accessible and it can be that a simplified form is also easier to interpret. The phrase 'it is said that you did (this)' or 'the prosecutor says that' is not so precise in legal terms but it gets the nub of the message across.

4. 'DVD', an abbreviation for Digital Video Disc, may not be a sufficient description to someone not familiar with the term.
5. 'Do you understand?' is not the best way of eliciting whether a listener has comprehended what has been said. Most people say 'yes' even when they have not understood and particularly where they are nervous or bewildered. Open questions are preferable.
6. 'Indicate'. What precisely does that mean in this context?
7. 'Guilty'. In Youth Courts the simpler, 'do you admit or deny doing this?' is used. The notion of guilt can be complex, especially where individuals come from a background where the legal and religious frameworks are close and guilt refers more explicitly to a moral dimension.
8. 'Proceed' could be expressed more informally as 'go ahead' where appropriate.
9. Terms such as 'magistrate', 'crown court', 'judge' and indeed 'clerk' describe particular roles and functions that need to be explained beforehand by the defendant's lawyer or the court lawyer.
10. 'The facts are given to the court'. By whom? It is essential that there is also a prior understanding of court procedures. The best person to give those facts is someone who is legally qualified, not the interpreter.

Interpreters notice the significant difference when they have worked with lawyers trained to explain procedures to defendants before a hearing, and with court lawyers and others who are conscious of the intercultural process. Interpreters have then been able to focus upon their own task, safe in the knowledge that others are doing theirs. Where small, or even large, cultural or communicative knots appear, they can be recognised earlier and more easily and everyone can contribute to disentangling them.

Approaches to training

Each public service discipline and organisation is responsible for training its own members and staff. They will routinely offer in-service training so that they can be up-to-date with new developments. Many, such as doctors and lawyers, have formal annual continuing professional development programmes that must be followed to preserve professional registration.

Training in how to work across languages and cultures varies considerably across and within countries. There are those, including on occasion interpreters who have been acting outside the strict confines of their role and are reluctant to devolve those responsibilities to qualified legal and medical professionals, who will disrespectfully suggest that public service personnel cannot or will not be trained in the necessary skills. But such training has proved to be simple and inexpensive to carry out and useful in practice. Public service personnel do not have to know the intricacies of how languages work any more than interpreters and translators need to know how to remove an appendix or investigate a crime. Each discipline has to know just sufficient about the others' role and expertise to be mutually supportive and complementary.

Fortunately, members of public service disciplines are used to being trained to work together: service is provided by multidisciplinary teams. For example, judges, lawyers and police officers know each other's roles in court; doctors, nurses, physiotherapists and pharmacists recognise and respect each other's expertise while providing health care. They have been trained to do this from the start and develop their skills in this during their day-to-day professional practice.

So the basic concept of training in interdisciplinary and complementary good practice is established. Its implementation in respect of language and culture is slowly being carried out in many countries. The combination of three teaching strategies has proved to be useful in training magistrates and local authority officers in the U.K:

- participation of public service personnel in interpreter training (see Chapter 4)
- direct classroom training
- development of skills on the job, under supportive supervision and mentoring (see Chapter 8).

Team teaching has proved helpful in all three strategies. The combination of an interpreter or translator working with the particular service's own trainers signals the engagement of the service in this aspect of their training. The service's own trainers can provide excellent practice-based scenarios and teaching materials. They also know how procedures may best be carried out in the context of their own discipline. The team approach also acts as a multiplier in that the service trainer is more likely to integrate points from this aspect into other areas of training.

Positive approaches are required. Public service personnel may have been dealing with speakers of other languages for some time, without qualified linguists, without really understanding how to work with interpreters and translators or across cultures and without informed support in this aspect of their work. These professional situations may therefore have become associated with anxiety, stress, sometimes guilt and even accompanied by a measure of self-justification to mitigate the guilt. Instead, those who work in the public services need to be provided with the skills to gain professional satisfaction and enjoyment of this aspect of their work.

Sets of skills required by public service personnel

A general desire to be helpful may be useful, but it is unlikely to produce effective delivery of expertise. A practical grounding in five sets of skills is needed, underpinned by a sound understanding of the relevant principles, to enable staff effectively to:

- communicate within a shared language and culture
- communicate through a shared language but without a shared culture
- communicate through interpreters
- work with translators
- deliver appropriate and effective service working across cultures.

As with any other set of professional skills, it is for the profession itself to ensure that strategies are in place for training, assessment, accountability, continuing development, support and supervision. It is demanding to work across language and culture, where even greater care than usual is needed. More on this will be set out in Chapter 8 (service delivery).

Language specialists invited to contribute to in-service training of the employees in any public service may wish to consider including the following incremental approach in their teaching strategies, although these will obviously vary according to the requirements of the particular public service, individual teaching styles and the type of participant. Each set of skills is addressed below from the point of view of training.

Communicate within a shared language and culture

Public service employees have been used to communicating through a shared language and culture all their working lives. In fact they have often been doing it so well, they may be unusually disconcerted when they face someone with whom they do not share a language or culture and may not know why.

It is therefore useful to deconstruct these skills for two reasons. The first is to affirm existing good communications skills, by making explicit some of the processes, which they already follow well intuitively. The second is to then extend those insights to enable additional communication strategies to be accommodated. It is not unlike the process motorists go through when driving a car in another country that requires them to drive on the other side of the road. To begin with they are conscious of being vividly aware of challenging each action, instead of being able to drive instinctively. Each decision is taken consciously and anxiously. But soon they adapt and drive as intuitively as ever.

From a socio-cultural point of view, an important component of successful communication is understanding non-verbal signals, particularly visual signals such as facial expressions and gestures (kinesics) and tactile signals such as bodily contact and distance between interlocutors (proxemics). Reading off 'indicators' is a highly developed skill among the best public service professionals, who have an intuitive grasp of non-verbal clues within their own culture. In a training situation, these skills can be explored by asking the class participants to 'read off' the trainer's own indicators, drawing also on other clues taken from the context such as clothing and general appearance:

- age
- marital status
- place of birth
- schooling
- religion
- favourite music e.g. Bach, Mantovani or heavy metal
- favourite type of restaurant e.g. Thai, French, Indian
- social attitudes e.g. the role of women in society.

The specific choice of questions is not important, so long as they can illustrate how much can and can't be deduced just by looking at someone and the point at which inferences are likely to become less accurate.

The next stage is to encourage the participants, without speaking, to answer the same questions about each other from the non-verbal signs. This is especially illuminating if they do not know one another, and the answers can be checked for accuracy during a coffee break. It can be interesting and useful to reflect upon the effect of indicators. For example, how teenagers experiment with their image and the effect that has on others and how they are perceived, or how actors can adopt a character by subtly changing their walk, their facial expressions and gestures, their hairstyle or their clothes.

The production of speech from planning to execution – or 'encoding of a message' – is a complex process which has been extensively studied in psycholinguistics. That is not our perspective here. Of much greater import are the sociolinguistics and pragmatic aspects of language use which reflect different ways of conveying the same proposition. Effective communication by public service employees such as police officers or nurses may depend on their ability to accommodate their utterances to their interlocutors and the situation, depending on shared knowledge, varying their use of linguistic features such as vocabulary, grammar and pronunciation, as well as so-called prosodic features such as rate of speaking and loudness, and paralinguistic features such as timbre or voice quality.

To raise awareness of such factors, training exercises can require the same incident to be described in different ways. Discussions can then focus on why it sounds strange when something said in an informal register, perhaps during a drunken disagreement, is reported *verbatim* in the formal context of a courtroom. Coping with non-standard varieties of the public service employee's language also needs to be covered and, of course, the extent to which such varieties are mutually intelligible. Stress, in the sense of which syllables in a word are emphasised relative to others and how changes in stress can change meaning as in '*Don't* do that', 'Don't *do* that' and 'Don't do *that*', also needs to be discussed. The tones of voice that nuance meaning are a fruitful source of discussion. The English word 'quite' is a good example. Said with clipped tones and without a smile, it can indicate strong disapproval rather than plain agreement. The gestures, facial expressions and body language that accompany messages, or are used as the only means of expressing a message, provide further discussion.

The order of information giving and the effect of relationships and context can be dealt with by, for example, suggesting that participants think how they might give the same news to a range of people. This might be that they are going skiing at Christmas, and consider how they would impart this information to their mother, employer, colleague and the next-door neighbour, who they hope will take care of their house.

Examples of turn-taking at meetings and on social occasions, which can be signalled by both verbal and prosodic and paralinguistic means, as well as gestures, facial expressions and body language provide further interesting insights into communication. Who listens to whom and why? Who manages to get their message across and why? Analysing a video recording of a meeting or a social occasion can be particularly informative, as it provides the opportunity to look objectively at the reasons why, for example, there are those who can never manage to get their turn, although potentially they may have something interesting to say; how there are those who manage not to cede the floor; how power games are played out through non-verbal, as well as verbal communication; and how intercultural factors may affect what is happening at different levels (see next section).

'Restricted languages' (after the British linguist J. R. Firth, 1890–1960) or, from a more recent perspective, 'languages for special purposes', are an important feature of communications in public service domains, dealing as they do with communication in constrained contexts, in which individuals have sufficient background in common to enable them to express complex messages in a few words. So members of the same profession use acronyms and phrases often not comprehensible to those outside their profession or discourse community. Less formally, Firth's notion of restricted language can be understood as the kind of shorthand language sometimes used within family groups and based on an incident with which all are familiar e.g. 'He's just doing a Bertie', where Bertie is a child who misbehaved on a given occasion when frustrated. One way of illustrating the phenomenon of restricted language is to ask participants to analyse and discuss the particular difficulties of understanding a text used in a specialist domain, such as a tenancy agreement or a computer manual or the regulations of an unfamiliar sport – such as curling or lacrosse.

Thought should also be given to the optimum ways of communicating with people who are not deaf but are hard-of-hearing. Many elderly people, for example, have hearing difficulties. Conducting the conversation in a good light, face-to-face in a quiet place and using simple, clear messages can make a difference to the success of the communicative exchange.

Public service professionals often have a good intuitive grasp of how utterances are understood (i.e. decoded) and how to monitor mutual understanding. Listening to and understanding what their clients or patients are saying should be one of the things they do best in their own language. Experience shows that monitoring understanding includes an appreciation of the fact that asking open questions can elicit confirmation of comprehension better than simply asking whether someone has understood, and that non-verbal signals such as eye contact or nodding can sometimes serve the same purpose.

Most public service professionals, as indicated in this section, have a good intuitive grasp of communicative strategies from production to comprehension in their own language and culture. Most have been trained how to break good news and bad news, and many are also highly skilled in interview techniques. In their training they can be encouraged to explore these intuitions within a systematic framework in a thought-provoking and enjoyable way with an emphasis on awareness-raising rather than theoretical constructs. The aim is to provide a sufficient basis for extension into communicating across cultures with the professional help of interpreters and translators.

Communicate through a shared language but without a shared culture

This section of the training introduces participants to cultural differences within the same speech community, such as communication between a British English native speaker doctor and a patient recently arrived from the Indian subcontinent with a high standard of English as a second language. This can often be done by revisiting the stages of communication previously studied in the context of same language/culture and looking at how each stage can be affected by a bicultural setting. The English doctor and the Indian patient may both be able to speak English fluently but may not communicate successfully unless they can accommodate the cultural gaps. The ability to be truly bicultural and bilingual is rare.

In the commercial and diplomatic worlds, individuals about to embark upon dealings with a particular country can attend preliminary courses that give them a background understanding of the history, cultural and courtesy conventions, business processes and language of that country. Such an approach is not possible for public service employees because as we have seen, some 300 languages are spoken in a city like London as well as English. In addition, a large proportion of those people will represent the linguistic and cultural shifts and mix common in today's global village. These may include individuals with, for example, an African father, who studied medicine at the Sorbonne, and an Indonesian mother who is working in London as an economist for an American international firm. There exists what are known as the 'culture rich kids' who are blessed with access to three or more languages and cultures, and can use any of them adeptly according to the situation they find themselves in. At the other end of the scale, there are also those struggling between two cultures and languages without a full command of either.

Various layers of culture also need to be considered, including for example, the culture of the individuals concerned and the institutional and professional culture of a particular public service, with its own systems, procedures and terminology. The public service employee and the other-language speaking member of the public are unlikely to have an equal understanding of the subject matter. A middle aged Spanish man consulting a doctor about the pain in his chest, by definition, knows less about medicine than the doctor. Indeed, the patient may not know the basic and relevant anatomy, physiology and terminology in any language. The pregnant Chinese woman consulting the midwife is in the same situation; she may not know the qualifications and role of the midwife, and the midwife may not know much, or anything, about the patient's background. Both the Spanish and Chinese patients do, however, know how they feel and are aware of their own perceptions, needs and attitudes. More information has to be exchanged between the patients and the health care staff than in monocultural situations in order to produce viable outcomes.

Different conventions for conducting conversations may also be in evidence, with respect to conversational moves such as turn-taking, for instance. Research into turn-taking conventions reveals many problems potentially leading to communication breakdown. FitzGerald (2003:111), for instance, reports that there is 'much evidence' that 'different turn-taking styles and the distribution of talk are culture-bound' and that '[c]ulturally-influenced features such as a preference for discrete turns or simultaneous talk, length of pauses between turns, length of turn and contrasting attitudes to silence and verbal self-expression may lead to difficulties in intercultural communication'.

Public service staff, such as health carers, may themselves come from a variety of cultural and language backgrounds. A doctor may be a second-generation immigrant, and may or may not have a full command of, say, the Punjabi language spoken by his parents, or an understanding of the culture of someone who has recently arrived from western Pakistan or Lahore. It is increasingly common, in the diplomatic, commercial and public service arenas, that communication happens through a *lingua franca*, such as English or Russian. But neither interlocutor may possess a cultural background associated with that language (see Ife 2005: 291–4 for a useful summary).

In the public service context, staff cannot predict who is going to appear in need of their help or what cultural, linguistic, social or educational backgrounds they may have, or indeed, expect to be familiar with them. Therefore, simple and well-understood coping strategies are needed for the public services, which can be improved and fine-tuned with experience.

Reading indicators across a culture is challenging. Each summer, in the market place in the university town of Cambridge, England, well-meaning American tourists are rumoured to press coins into the palms of scruffy looking elderly gentlemen who happen to be distinguished academics and who, not wishing to be discourteous, murmur polite thanks. Assumptions can be risky. Every individual has a unique cultural background arising from his or her upbringing, education, work and life experiences. This can be demonstrated by inviting participants to deduce what they can from the same set of questions, on age and so on mentioned earlier in this chapter, about people of different backgrounds and to answer them on the basis of non-verbal clues alone. Simple matters like age can be difficult to assess; marital status equally so, when men in particular may or may not wear wedding rings; schooling and tertiary education, likely preferences in music, food and so on are not so evident. Religion, which is not relevant in many cultures, is very relevant in others.

In diplomatic and commercial contexts, formal and informal social gatherings are often integral to the job, and help those present to get a sense of who others are in terms of interests, hobbies, attitudes and sense of humour. In the public services, that approach is impossible: the doctor and the lawyer are not in a position to engage socially with every client with whom he or she does not share a culture.

The simplest route forward is quietly and sensitively to ask the individual concerned what one needs to know and to give information about oneself. People who are accustomed to living in countries other than their own can also become adept at providing the necessary clues. At times, that can be clumsy for a variety of linguistic and cultural reasons, and produce unintended dissonances. Intercultural grace demands generosity of spirit as well as an understanding of what is really happening.

There is also the matter of the degree of shared language. Those speaking the shared language as a second language may be less than fluent and lack in areas of terminology. Native fluency is rare in such cases. Even an advanced user is unlikely to know the terminology around Caesarean sections or immunisation without further training. Nor, just as importantly, may they be informed about the usual processes about hospital visiting, and may need much more background information than usually has to be given to a native speaker. In South America, for instance, it is customary for family members and friends to sit with and take care of the patient in the hospital day and night (see, for instance, Márquez-Reiter 2005 on caregiver services), whereas in western European hospitals, comparatively strict visiting hours are in operation. In addition, the non-verbal communication used may be based in one or both cultures and cannot be accurately decoded.

Putting messages into words therefore requires careful thought when there is not a fully shared culture. Once apprised of the principles, class participants can enjoy practising reformulating some of the phrases they use every day to suit the range of individuals from different backgrounds whose indicators, language fluency and understanding of the relevant service they tried to interpret earlier. In such exercises, experience shows that the use of clear, simple and unambiguous language and a clear structure for information are a good foundation for effective communication, subject, of course, to careful feedback and monitoring.

The good communicators in a training group usually quickly adapt and develop a pace and awareness that enables them to communicate accurately and smoothly, accommodating gaps as they go, testing mutual comprehension and building appropriate relationships. Some may even be conscious that having a more explicit understanding of how communication processes work interculturally will help to improve their communication with clients from their own culture and speech community (see, for instance, the CILT project to develop *National Occupational Standards for Intercultural Working* in the UK, at http://www.cilt. org.uk/standards/intercultural.htm).

Communicate through interpreters

The first two stages can provide the foundation for teaching this next set of skills. The interpreting process is integrated into the communication process between the primary interlocutors, i.e. the public service employee and the patient or client. Questions and debate quickly begin and usually include the following:

Whose indicators are read by the interlocutors – the other interlocutor's or the interpreter's?

It is not helpful to read the interpreter's indicators because the message should be formulated according to the interlocutor's individual educational, social and cultural background. The interpreter will follow in the footprints of each speaker; if the interlocutors do not accommodate each other, the message may, for example, be in the wrong register. Interpreters should not change register or adapt what the speaker is saying to ensure comprehension because they may not be aware whether a particular register or approach has been chosen deliberately by the public service professional or the patient, for example. What the interpreter may do is to alert the parties involved to a potential misunderstanding, and the possible reasons for that, to allow interlocutors the opportunity to adjust their register or to clarify what they are saying.

What is the background of the interlocutor?

Given the difficulty of reading indicators accurately across a culture, it is advisable to ask the listener, through the interpreter, for the necessary relevant information. It is important that, for example, a nurse, doctor, social worker or lawyer knows the background of the person they are dealing with, in order for them to formulate their message appropriately and to provide an effective service. A science graduate is likely to understand, via an interpreter, a relatively technical explanation about an X-ray process while a forester may not. Equally, the other-language speaker can ask questions of the public service staff in order to understand their backgrounds.

What is the best way to formulate a message for interpreting?

Again, experience shows that using clear, simple and unambiguous language and structuring information logically is likely to be effective. Saying precisely what is meant, without euphemisms or circumlocutions, and speaking in a clear audible voice, at an even pace are also important, remembering that the interlocutors and the interpreter are also decoding non-verbal signals.

How does a speaker know if the interpreter has understood the message?

Interpreters are trained to ask for clarification if they have not fully grasped the meaning of what they have been asked to interpret.

How long can the interlocutors talk before pausing for consecutive interpretation?

In order to raise awareness of this question in training, a short-term memory test can be used. A suitable short paragraph (containing about 14 factual points) from a newspaper is read out, and the group is invited to listen without taking notes before writing down what has been said. The original text can then be re-read for them to check their own accuracy. Interpreters are trained to develop their short-term memory and to use notes as aides-memoires. However, pauses for interpreting after two or three sentences, or at the end of a unit of information, are recommended. That enables the exchange to gather its own pace and dynamic, without parties having to wait too long for speech in a language they understand. Participants are taught not to pause mid-sentence because the interpreter is left without the complete unit of information and, furthermore, in a language such as German the verb may occur at the end of a sentence. When a speaker has overlooked the need to pause at appropriate moments, interpreters will alert him or her to the fact.

Simultaneous interpreting may also be used on occasion in a PSI context. Instead of the glass-fronted booths used in international conferences with supporting technology relaying the interpreted speech through headphones to the delegates, in the public service context interpreters whisper a simultaneous interpretation or *chuchotage*[1]. Speakers can accommodate this by speaking at a pace that allows the interpreter to keep up.

Mutual understanding can be monitored through the usual open questions through the interpreter such as, 'Mr X, just to be sure we understand one another, how many times a day are you going to take these pills and how many each time?' The other party must be given an opportunity to also clarify their understanding. If there is a missed cultural inference, when it has been assumed that information is within a person's frame of reference and it is not, the interpreter will alert the parties to the fact and then interpret the explanations.

The teaching session can be interleaved by a number of activities such as shadowing, in which participants are asked to whisper to a colleague the accurate and complete meaning of a short talk while it is being spoken and in the same language but using different words.

Participants in the training course normally come to realise other implications for the planning of an interpreted exchange. They come to appreciate that they should, where possible, make advance preparations in terms of briefing the interpreter on terminology and procedures to be involved in the event, that they should allow additional time for the appointment and make sure it takes place in a quiet place so that audibility is not affected by noisy disruptions.

A series of short interpreted role plays can consolidate what has been learnt and bring it to life. The scenarios should be carefully prepared to reflect day-to-day real-life situations such as antenatal care, school parents' evenings or even complete mock trials. The public service staff play themselves. An interpreter interprets between them and a colleague from the same language group. Critiques should follow the usual pattern described in Chapter 4 on training interpreters but, for these occasions, more emphasis is placed on the public service staff's performance.

It is interesting to observe how quickly public service staff can adapt to working with an interpreter, and how their increased awareness of the interpreting process discourages them in the future from using as interpreters family and friends, passing kitchen staff or colleagues who cannot do much more than order a meal in another language. They are also made aware of the potential risk to themselves and their service that comes from not employing qualified interpreters. The professional reputations and careers of the members of public service disciplines, such as doctors, nurses, lawyers and social workers are based upon the professional decisions they make, which in turn are based upon the quality of information available to them. Without accurate information exchange, all the parties involved are exposed to risk.

Such in-service training also tactfully establishes the role of interpreters as fellow professionals in their own right. Part of the professional skill of an interpreter is to facilitate communication between others without intruding, creating a kind of professional invisibility. Indeed, one anecdote tells of doctors holding conferences on 'communication' without inviting applied linguists, whose discipline centres on the subject (see, for example, Channell 2007). Doctors solemnly gave papers to one another about, what is to them, newly discovered territory. The observation, by amused linguists, that they were thinking of holding a conference on brain surgery and not inviting any doctors, but thought better of it, met with offended surprise among the medical fraternity.

Working with Translators

Some guidelines have already been published (see Corsellis 1995) and disseminated within the public services. They are likely to include the following suggestions for the public service employee.

Assessing the text to be translated

The person commissioning a translation should first assess the text to be translated and its context, in order to be in a position to brief the translator efficiently. Translators will need to know first of all what language the text is written in and what language it is to be translated into, so that they can ensure that their working languages match what is needed.

Then they will need to know what sort of document it is, such as a letter, information leaflet or a professional report; its length, if possible, number of words; the degree of technical or specialist terminology and whether there are any problems with legibility.

Information should be given as to the purpose of the text and whether, for example, it is intended to be a polished text for publication or an accurate but less polished text for immediate in-house only use. How the translation is to be presented is the next step, including whether camera-ready copy is needed. Layout needs to be considered, especially in those languages where the source language is written from left to right and the target language is written from right to left, or vice versa. In such cases, illustrations, photographs, maps and annotations can too easily end up disassociated from the explanatory texts. Colours have different significance in different cultures.

With that information as a basis, realistic deadlines can be discussed. Before contacting the translators, agreements should have been made with the appropriate authority in the service responsible for expenditure so that the translator's fees can be paid within 30 days.

It should be noted that deaf people who were born deaf may not be fully literate. Consideration could be given to video letters where they are fluent in sign language.

Engaging and commissioning a translator

There is generally not a good level of understanding in the public services in recognising when they need the assistance of a translator. In some cases, of course, an interpreter may be asked to undertake some short and straightforward written and sight translation during an assignment. In other cases, those without the relevant training may be asked to undertake such tasks, or even the translation of longer, more complex texts. There is much use of the word 'only', as in 'this is only a short text', 'only for the patient', 'only for the doctor' or 'only for the notice board'. The inference is that anyone with a slim grasp of another language can do the job and anecdotes abound about the consequences. Once there is recognition of the need for qualified translators, public service employees may, understandably, not know where or how to contact a qualified translator. The telephone directory or random web-surfing can be misleading if they do not know what they are looking for.

The contact details of qualified translators who belong to a professional language body with suitable admission criteria and have promised to adhere to a code of conduct can usually be obtained from that body. So long as translators have secure IT systems, it may not matter if they do not live locally.

When an appropriate translator has been located, he or she should be provided with the results of the assessment of the text as set out above. The translator should be supplied with the name and contact details of who is commissioning them. The translator is likely also to wish to have the name and contact details of someone who is an expert in the subject matter or the author of the original texts, in case there are ambiguities or technical terms to be clarified, if the specialist is not the commissioner.

Discussions should take place between translators, and the author or expert engaging them, as to how to handle terms for which there may be no equivalent in the other language. In formal texts, using footnotes may be the best approach. In other sorts of texts, explanations within the text may be better.

Collaborations over pre-editing the source text may be sensible in situations where it is vital that the reader understands and follows every detail. Mixing formula bottle-feeds for babies, administering medication and instructions for individuals on bail are obvious examples. A text about mixing baby formula, for example, can benefit from a pre-editing process where the text is adapted, often at the suggestion of the translator, to respond to the likely social, cultural and educational background of the young parents. This is done through a collaboration of insights from people in the best position to give them. Then health care staff and translator may collaborate on piloting the draft translation with two or three mothers to make sure that the text is clear, unambiguous and can be followed safely and easily so that the formulas are mixed correctly and bottles and teats are suitably prepared and stored.

Public service information letters, notices and leaflets that require or invite readers to follow a certain course of action should be checked by the public service concerned to make sure that it is practicable. There is no point, for example, in giving a notice to other-language speakers serving a community sentence order, requiring them to telephone their probation officer if they cannot attend an appointment or be at risk of arrest, unless there is someone who speaks his or her language on duty to receive the call. It is equally unhelpful to invite vulnerable other-language speakers to visit the social services department at such and such an address if they cannot know how to get there and may be unable to communicate with anyone there once they arrive. Dedicated language answering services and known times when bilingual staff or interpreters are on duty can be a solution and should be publicised.

Where strict security arrangements are needed, it may be best for suitable space and equipment to be made available for the translator to carry out the task in a building of the commissioning service.

Two copies of contracts must be agreed and co-signed in advance. These should include not only arrangements for fees but also for checking, proofreading, presentation and when, where and how the completed translation is to be delivered (see, for instance, the new European standard on the provision of translation services BS EN 15038:2006).

Suggestions for managers

If the public service has a multilingual constituency, translations are likely to be needed on a regular basis. It is therefore desirable to put in place policies, budgets and structures to accommodate them, as well as a database of information about the other languages needed and the numbers of people speaking them.

There are three broad groups of translation events to be dealt with:

- Large-scale activities, such as programmes for immunisation of children against polio, small pox, diphtheria, measles and so on: information and explanations have to reach every parent in the area or the country. Omission of one language group could not only have serious consequences for that group but also leave a potential source of disease that could affect the whole community. Where there are groups of other-language speakers, information leaflets and other relevant texts should be translated in relation to such common activities as antenatal clinics, crime prevention and environmental welfare.
- A single matter involving a sequence of service agencies and organisations over a period of time: this happens, for instance, in the criminal justice system where a single case can progress from the offence, through investigation, to pre-trial hearings, medical or psychological reports, to court hearings, to the implementation of sentence. The case could concern trafficking in drugs or people and involve the need for translation of evidential material from a number of countries through which the people or drugs had been smuggled. Victim and witness support would have been needed throughout, with all the associated written explanations and information given.
- One-off occasions when, for example, a lengthy letter from a client to a social worker has to be translated.

There are approaches that can maximise cost-effectiveness and quality. In the UK, there have been instances where a number of local authorities, or even a number of departments within local authorities, have had similar documents translated with insufficient resources that has resulted in poor translations. It would have been better had they combined their efforts for a more cost-effective and better result.

So there are economies of scale to be had for the first two groups of translations, with forethought and planning. Modern IT systems allow for qualified translators to be contacted and for larger print runs of common texts that allow for local addition of relevant maps and addresses. It is, of course, a challenge to quantify cost-effectiveness, or what would have happened in the absence of translations and how much that would have cost.

Working Across Cultures

Interpreted role plays, as part of communication training based on real-life scenarios, are likely to have given public sector professionals such as doctors, nurses, lawyers, probation officers and dieticians cause to reflect upon how they provide their service across cultures. While people with language skills can contribute to the training of public service employees, make suggestions on certain points and be supportive, this is primarily a matter that colleagues from other professions have to develop for themselves. Many already have existing areas of sound expertise, gained as a result of working with particular groups of clients from different cultural backgrounds. Few will have an underpinning structure for recording and disseminating those skills, nor may those skills be integrated within the formal framework of their career development.

Health care staff, for example, need to develop an understanding of different but valid notions of health and healing if they are to serve a multicultural client group. Medical anthropology has an established and valuable body of knowledge that is too little known among practitioners. Dieticians should be fully aware of a range of culinary traditions and how to adapt them for clinical purposes. The legal services should be aware of different concepts of natural justice. Social services should be cognizant of, for example, different family structures and kin groupings. The significant life events such as births and deaths, and the rites of passage such as weaning babies, teenage angst and care of the elderly are all surrounded by needs, perceptions, attitudes and taboos that can differ not only between individuals but also between cultures.

It is not being suggested here, for instance, that a country's legal or health care system should be altered fundamentally, but rather that these systems work with the grain of an individual's culture and thereby better fulfil their aims. It is a matter of widening existing skills and flexible approaches to extend them to a wider range of starting points. The legal system can, for example, carry out community-based sentencing to help prevent a young man re-offending while helping him to resolve his confusions of being caught between cultures. Teaching children in schools in ways that recognise and accommodate the different learning traditions they may have come from is the starting point to enabling them to gain control of their own learning. Understanding that parents may have varying attitudes to their daughters participating in sport and going on school trips enables the school and parents to negotiate strategies they all feel comfortable with and which are in the best interests of the child.

Where training has not been provided, the lack of these skills and strategies on the part of the public services is a source of frustration for interpreters. They can be providing the best possible standards of interpreting and still the service provided is inappropriate and ineffective – not to mention a waste of tax-payers' money. Interpreters can be placed in impossible situations. Public services can try to offload the intercultural service delivery onto the interpreter in ways which pressure the interpreters to step outside their role, cause them to disobey their own professional code of conduct and thereby put themselves at risk of disciplinary procedures and potential litigation, also putting the service and its clients at risk. Incidents have been reported, for example, in which doctors have asked interpreters to take medical case histories, police officers have asked interpreters to take witness statements and midwives have asked interpreters to give a talk on antenatal care or visit a home and report back on the health of a mother and baby – all on the basis that interpreters have interpreted during a number of similar events before. One can see that, at first glance, this could be tempting as interpreters are bicultural, speak both languages and probably know the procedures. However, it should be self-evident that interpreters are not qualified to do any of these tasks and the risk to clients as well as to their own professional reputation would be high.

Experience has shown, however, that where public service staff are trained to accommodate cultures the standards of service improve. Interestingly, it also appears to improve within same cultural situations as the need to explore overtly an individual's needs, perceptions and attitudes, and seek to meet them, becomes a more routine part of a process.

Guidelines for good practice when working with interpreters

Members of regulated professional disciplines are obliged to observe codes of ethics, as we have seen in relation to public service interpreters and translators (Chapter 3). The implementation of factors within such codes are promoted through guidelines to good practice, which in the case of public service employees in hospitals, for instance, include instructions on how to use a piece of equipment, such as an X-ray machine, and how best to administer medication, with all the checks on correct dosages and so on. Such guidelines promote consistency, standards and protection of good practice. They are often available at two levels. National guidelines will set out the core. These may be added to at a local level so that, for example, where the national guidelines will set out the need to ensure that information is provided, the local guidelines will add the details of where. Guidelines are also responsive and, while still observing the codes of conduct, can be updated and changed. New guidelines will be developed to deal with new situations. They form the basis of in-service training and are usually made easily accessible in the workplace so that they may be quickly referred to as reminders, for it is a fact of life that additional procedures are often needed at the most inconvenient and busy time.

In this context, a guide to good practice is needed for working with interpreters, mirroring and complementing the interpreters' guidelines to good practice described in Chapter 3 (see Chapter 6 for the guidelines for working with translators).

Most guidelines should include the following generic factors:

Recognising when an interpreter is needed

An interpreter is needed when the public service employee and the member of the public do not share sufficient common ground linguistically to conduct the matter in hand properly and effectively to the standards required for good practice. That includes avoiding potential risk as a result of miscommunication, to the member of the public, the public service employee and the service. Professional considerations are paramount but time and cost to the taxpayer exert pressure on the public services. Time and money can be saved by making the right decisions about communication strategies at the outset.

Mostly it is self-evident that an interpreter is needed but it can be a more complex decision. It can be hard to admit to language limitations. It should be made clear that the need for communication is equally shared. The public service employee needs to communicate as much as the member of the public. It is not only the latter's 'problem'. The decision as to whether or not to call an interpreter is therefore a shared one but, where there is any doubt, the public service employee should have the right to call one. Both interlocutors need to understand that registered interpreters are bound by their code to be impartial and to keep confidences. They can also be told that it is acceptable for the interpreter to act as a language support (often called standby interpreting), if required. That is, the conversation can be conducted so far as possible in a common language, with the interpreter providing unfamiliar words or phrases where necessary. Where there are cost implications for the service, line managers should be consulted if necessary.

It requires a high level of fluency to communicate accurately in a second or foreign language, especially when one is anxious, sick or frightened; public service employees are not trained to assess competence in other languages and it may be difficult for them to decide whether someone is really able to proceed without an interpreter. Some clients or patients may appear, in the first instance, to have a fluent grasp of the other language and speak convincingly. Indeed they may be fluent within specific areas such as relaying their name and address, simple shopping or in their work context, but they can soon be out of their depth in another context. It can be revealing to ask open questions requiring use of less common language such as 'What did the doctor say about your *condition* last time?'

Literacy is another factor to be taken into consideration because there can be few public services without documentation and forms to be completed and signed. This includes significant texts such as witness statements, operation consent forms and medical prescriptions. There are those who can speak a language fluently but who do not have comparable standards of literacy. They may not even be literate in their first language: Education is often among the first casualties of war and economic hardship. Some languages have no written form, such as Mirpuri spoken in Mirpur, Pakistan. There may be no correlation between the perceived importance of an event and the degree of linguistic complexity involved. A high court hearing involving a straightforward guilty plea may be linguistically simpler than the language used in a downtown neighbourhood dispute, where the interpreter(s) may have to accommodate nuance, speed, range of registers, oaths, threats, disconnected speech and everyone talking or shouting at once. In addition, what may start out as a simple interchange, such as a request for a repeat prescription, may turn into a more complicated one if, for example, a patient begins to talk about the side effects of the medication.

Clearly, it is helpful if the need for an interpreter is known in advance of an event. By definition, the members of the public concerned are rarely able to provide this prior notice themselves. There is a need, therefore, for liaison between the various parties within and between services. Police or lawyers should alert the courts, general practice doctors should alert hospitals, courts should alert doctors from whom they want medical reports. Receptionists and booking clerks should note special language needs on the information lists attached to each file. Some services have devised a special file form for interpreting for that purpose. It includes note of the specific language or dialect required and which interpreter was employed on each occasion, although the matter of language identification is not always a straightforward one.

Language identification

The first and essential point is to ensure a language match between the interpreter and the other-language speaker. More often than not, one can simply ask someone and they will know enough of the common language to say, for example, ' French' or 'Russian'. But it is not always as easy as that. There is no reason why public service employees should be experts in language identification, but a few simple pointers can help.

Asking where individuals come from by asking them to point to a map for example, may be a start but not always helpful for two principal reasons. Firstly and increasingly, an individual may have been born in one country but left it in infancy and been educated in another country. Secondly, there may be a number of languages spoken within one country such as in Switzerland, India and China.

It helps to ask individuals what their best, or preferred, language is, as proficiency may vary across a range of languages. The reasons for certain choices also need to be understood. A language such as Urdu may be chosen as the preferred language as it has a higher status than a language in which the patient or client is more proficient. Or it might be assumed that it is easier to find an Urdu interpreter than one for the patient's or client's best language.

If an educated guess can be made as to the language in question, it is possible to telephone an interpreter in that language to confirm the match. It is likely that, if the match is not accurate but related to the interpreter's working language, he or she may have suggestions as to which it is, and another interpreter in that language can be contacted. If security considerations demand it, the topics of the conversation between the interpreter and the other-language speaker can be restricted to the matter in hand and supervised.

Non-standard varieties of a language can be problematic to accommodate. It has often been said that public service interpreters have to be more than *bilingual*, in that they have to be able to comprehend the standard variety of both their working languages as well as any variety that may be spoken by individuals in either the public services or by the general public. For example, the underpinning cultural concepts and some of the terminology used by speakers of Gujarati from Gujarat may differ sufficiently from the Gujarati spoken by in East Africa, with the result that communication may be put at risk for those not fully familiar with those differences. Also, the informal register and terminology used in day-to-day situations are different from, say, the formal register used in courtrooms.

In addition, the shift and mix of language use across languages and generations can give the interpreter and the public service staff cause to tread carefully. Individuals can speak a combination of languages, where terms are used from two or more sources.

It is also perfectly reasonable for a British Asian interpreter living in London, for example, not to comprehend Glaswegian English fully or for a young speaker of standard Italian to be sure of all the fossilised varieties of Italian spoken in parts of Britain. Admission of professional limitations is part of the interpreters' code of conduct and they should declare it if they judge that effective mutual comprehension is not going to be possible. That judgement should be accepted by the public service staff. Pressure should not be brought to bear on the interpreter to accept an assignment because the language match is 'near enough'. The only exception when a complete language match might be foregone is, as an interim measure, on such occasions as a medical emergency when minutes are vital. In these circumstances it is recommended that there is a short written statement of the facts co-signed in advance.

Relying on information about an other-language speaker's country of origin to identify the right language can also lead to serious errors. In a recent case in the English Court of Appeal, Criminal Division, a conviction for causing death by dangerous driving was set aside on the grounds that the appellant, whose first language was Tetum, had been assigned an interpreter for Bahasa Indonesian, the official language of East Timor, the appellant's home country. It was the interpreter in this case who alerted the trial judge to the discrepancy as it became clear that the appellant had not understood important parts of the proceedings (*Regina* v. *Endenico Belo*).

Language identification where the speaker cannot be asked what language they use, such as when transcribing wire taps or in hostage situations, may require expert linguistic assistance. It is therefore wise to know where that assistance may be found in case it is needed quickly.

Locating an interpreter

Increasingly, there are language professional bodies and registers to be turned to, or suitable agencies that employ registered interpreters (see Chapter 6). Their members or registrants should have had prior assessment of their language and interpreting competence at an appropriate level, had security checks and be obliged to abide by a code of conduct or ethics (see Chapter 5). It may be that there are, as yet, insufficient numbers of qualified interpreters available in all the languages and geographical locations required. In which case people with the equivalent levels of skills, described in earlier chapters, need to be sought. Children should not be used as interpreters for obvious reasons.

It makes life very difficult indeed for the public services in countries where there are no such language professional bodies. That is probably the reason why the front line practitioners in the public services, such as police officers, nurses, doctors and judges, have been at the forefront of urging for their development.

Commissioning an interpreter[2]

Once a suitably qualified interpreter, with the correct language match, has been located, the following factors, which mirror the guidelines for interpreters in Chapter 5, should be discussed and agreed.

- The interpreter's availability at the date, time and location required and for the estimated duration of the assignment needs to be agreed. The public service practitioner should be aware that good interpreters do their best to be accommodating but that they have to manage a professional diary responsibly. It can be beneficial to negotiate dates, times and places to mutual advantage where that is possible, for a dental check-up, for example. On other occasions, such as a medical emergency, there can be no leeway.
- Also important are potential conflicts of interest. These mirror closely the principles that apply to anyone working as a public service professional, e.g. whether the other-language speaker is well known or related to the interpreter, or whether there are mutual financial interests.
- Travel arrangements also have to be made. How the location can best be reached, especially at night, any security arrangements to be observed, car-parking facilities and the person to be contacted on arrival. It is important that the appropriate people, such as security guards and receptionists, are warned of the interpreter's arrival so that they can be suitably welcomed and directed, etc.
- The name and details and telephone number of the staff member to be contacted in case of delay or other practical matters must be identified.
- Letters of agreement over fees, expenses and so forth should be completed in advance where a freelance interpreter is involved, and agreed with line managers. Elements to be covered are listed in Chapter 5. Failure to do so has the potential for future embarrassment and time-consuming negotiations.
- The name and file number of the other-language speaker is required to identify the assignment and, perhaps, to locate in a busy clinic.
- A briefing is required on relevant subject matter and procedures. Public service interpreters should, if well trained, have a background knowledge of the services they expect to work in and the main processes involved (see Chapter 4 on their training and assessment). No one, however, can know everything about such broad subjects as law and health care. Simply to be told that it is a routine appointment in an antenatal clinic, or a housing department, is likely to suffice

especially when the interpreter has worked there before. It is always worthwhile, however, for the interpreter to be briefed on the terminology and procedures likely to be encountered, to give an opportunity for questions. Public service staff who have been trained to work with interpreters learn to use their imagination. They will not say 'a court hearing about a motoring offence' but 'a court hearing involving defective brake linings, broken offside rear light and non-payment of vehicle excise licence'.

- Arrangements need to be made for the interpreter to study any texts that are to be used or referred to. These may include forms, letters, reports, and legal documents. It may be necessary to take security precautions on occasions and provide a room available for this purpose.

Preparing for an event that involves an interpreter

- Time should be set aside in advance for the event that accommodates the extra time arising from interpreting. Otherwise frustration arises when the hour normally set aside for a court hearing, or the ten minutes allowed for a doctor's consultation, expands.
- Acoustics should be checked because all the parties need to be able to hear one another very clearly. They will not do so if the road is being dug up outside the window, babies are screaming or the air conditioning is faulty. Any technology, such as microphones, must be checked to make sure it is working.
- Seating and positioning arrangements should be discussed with interpreters in advance. For example, where interpreting is between two people, the interpreter will normally sit equidistant between the two parties, rather than sitting by one person. In a court room they will sit or stand next to the other-language speaker and room has to be made for the interpreter in, or next to, the dock or witness stand. Where sign language interpreters are employed, they have to be positioned where they can hear and see all the parties likely to speak and where they and the deaf person can see one another clearly. Where there is a group discussion, involving one or two other-language speakers – such as a case conference – careful thought must be given to positioning.
- Public service participants in the event should know how to work with an interpreter and have read and understood the relevant guidelines to good practice for the purpose.
- Just before the event, public service employees should, where necessary, bring the interpreter up to date with any pertinent changes

that have taken place since the original commissioning, such as changes in the situation or the state of mind of the other-language speaker.

During the interpreted event

- Where this is the custom, on arrival interpreters will show their identity card to the appropriate public service member of staff. ID cards may have a photograph of the interpreter on the front, to avoid any misrepresentation as a result of perhaps a lost card and the word INTERPRETER in letters sufficiently large to be read across a room, so that everyone knows who they are. The interpreter's name and registration number are usually on the back, in case their privacy needs to be respected.
- Introductions should be made formally, through the interpreter, so that all the parties, including the other-language speaker, know who is present. Names and modes of address, where relevant, should be precise.
- Interpreters will normally introduce themselves last, to indicate they are not one of the principals. They will then set out their role for the benefit of the other-language speaker and include in their statement that they will:
  - interpret everything that is said to them
  - act impartially
  - observe confidentiality
  - intervene when they need clarification, accommodation of the interpreting process or to alert parties to potential misunderstanding or missed cultural inference. They will then interpret subsequent explanations
  - use direct rather than indirect speech

- The public service professional, such as a doctor, social worker or police officer, remains in charge of the event in the normal way, keeping a watchful eye on the communication process. With experienced interpreters and public service professionals, a comfortable rhythm is achieved. Pauses are made at the right moment for consecutive interpreting, anything to be interpreted simultaneously is spoken at a reasonable pace and any interpreter interventions are smoothly accommodated.
- Following introductions through the interpreter, the public service professional should, at the outset, clarify what is happening: the purpose of the event, what is going to happen and why, and encourage the other-language speaker to ask questions and when.

- If the event lasts longer than an hour, the interpreter should be given a short break in order to be able to maintain concentration.
- At the completion of the event, the conclusions of what has taken place should be summarised by the person leading it and the practicalities of any next steps, such as another appointment, clarified and set in motion; the other-language speaker should be given another opportunity to ask questions.

After the assignment

- The necessary arrangements must be made for the interpreter's fees to be paid.
- The interpreter will ask how to dispose of any confidential material they may have.
- File notes are completed. These should ensure that relevant, necessary and verifiable details as to language and culture acquired during the event are passed on to colleagues where appropriate.
- Any lessons to be learnt to promote better practice are recognised and absorbed.

Good practice guidelines for specific activities in the public services

Generic guidelines are not always sufficient when it comes to specific activities associated with particular public service tasks such as taking a witness statement in a police station. More specific guidelines are therefore required on occasion, partly to ensure that (in such a case, for example) legal requirements are met. The aims are to ensure national consistency of good practice and to avoid confusion.

Assessment of the public service practitioners' skills

It is not yet the norm for public service practitioners to have their skills assessed in working with interpreters and translators and across cultures. But it is generally recognised that it is only a matter of time before this takes place because of the need to provide an effective service to all, irrespective of language and culture where required.

It would be perfectly possible for these skills to be assessed, at a range of levels, through a combination of approaches such as on-the-job assessments, portfolios and short study projects. Clearly, a nationally recognised assessment would promote consistency, portability and potential career prospects.

Suggested activities

Consider what appropriate actions may be taken by interpreters if:

- the public service employee consistently forgets to use direct speech
- they are asked to wait in a clinic or court for much longer than was planned and they have a subsequent professional engagement
- they become aware that an aspect of service provision is culturally inappropriate and could cause offence.

Further reading

Cambridge, J. (2004) *Interpreting for the Public services Client: an Information booklet.* CILT North West Regional Languages Network.

Corsellis, A. (1997) 'Training needs of public personnel working with interpreters', in A. Carr, R. Roberts, A. Dufour and D. Steyn (eds) *The Critical Link 1. Interpreters in the Community.* Amsterdam: John Benjamins. 77–89.

Heaton-Armstrong, A., Shepherd, E., Gudjonsson, G. and Wolchover, D. (eds) (2006) *Witness Testimony – Psychological, Investigative and Evidential Perspectives.* Oxford: Oxford University Press.

Helman, C. G. (2001) *Culture, Health and Healing* (4th edition). Oxford: Oxford University Press.

Krause, I-B. (1989) 'Sinking Heart: A Punjabi Communication of Distress' *Soc. Sci. Med.* 29, 4, 563–73.

Meyer, B., Apfelbaum, B., Pöchhacker, F. and Bischoff, A. (2003) 'Analysing interpreted doctor-patient communication from the perspectives of linguistics, interpreting studies and health sciences', in L. Brunette, G. Bastian, I. Hemlin and H. Clarke (eds) *The Critical Link 3. Interpreters in the Community* (pp. 67–79). Amsterdam: John Benjamins.

Tebble, H. (2003) 'Training doctors to work effectively with interpreters', in L. Brunette, G. Bastian, I. Hemlin and H. Clarke (eds) *The Critical Link 3. Interpreters in the Community* (pp. 81–95). Amsterdam: John Benjamins.

Trompenars, F. and Hampden-Turner, C. (2001) *Riding the Waves of Culture.* London: Nicholas Brealey Publishing.

Websites

CILT (forthcoming) *National Occupational Standards for Intercultural Working* http://www.cilt.org.uk/standards/intercultural.htm (site visited 20 October 2007).

8
Management and Policy

The first rule of management is to enable others to succeed. Yet it is rare to find so far any multilingual country with both a consistent policy and complete, effective strategies for implementation of the delivery of public services to all, irrespective of language and culture. There may sometimes be legislation and statements of worthy aims but they are not enough without the training and structures to put them into practice on a national level. Or there may be pockets of trained Public Service Interpreters (PSIs) and Public Service Employees (PSEs) with relevant skills, but without a national policy and strategy for pulling them together to enable co-ordination, consistency and development.

This situation can be compared with that of interpreters and translators working in commercial fields where both policy and management strategies are more likely to be in place. Exporters, for example, provide goods and services overseas. They know how to conduct market research to find out about the languages their potential customers speak and about the customers' needs, perceptions and attitudes in relation to the product. Companies re-tool washing machines, for instance, so that the buttons are arranged for the convenience of the customers. They advertise their product so that the greatest number of people know about it and in ways that accommodate cultural perceptions, negotiate methods of supply, provide an after-sales service, conduct quality assurance strategies and then do more research and development to improve both the product and the processes for the future. They employ interpreters, translators and employees with second language skills, and the necessary other additional skills required at every stage. The company is likely to fail if any of these components are not properly attended to.

Managers of public services have a more difficult task to deliver a national or regional service to a multilingual and multicultural constituency and rarely have any specific training for this aspect of their work. Linguists with a range of expertise are at times invited to contribute to strategy on the basis of their linguistic and cultural insights.

The aim of this chapter is to make some practical suggestions about:

- Information needed about those requiring a service to inform future planning.
- Skills sets needed for the tasks to be done.
- Structures and strategies for incremental development.

Such activities should be set within a coherent national policy guidance[1] and management framework that enables public services to achieve the quality standards they aspire to, to diminish risk to their institutions and service users, and to promote cost-effectiveness.

Any implementation will depend upon opportunities and national systems and traditions. While there are examples of local good practice, national approaches in many countries tend to be fragmented, uncoordinated, ineffective and costly in terms of both human and financial resources. The reasons for any absence of coherent organisational focus are various and may include a witting or unwitting reluctance to cater for those who do not speak the language of the country (see Chapter 1).

As indicated in Chapter 1, recent reports in the UK national media indicate the strongly political and controversial nature of interpreting and translation provision in the public services, following a report by the government-initiated Commission for Integration and Cohesion that translation and interpreting services were discouraging non-English speakers from integrating with the majority language and culture. More often the reason for inaction is likely to be due to simple inertia where systems, designed for a monolingual constituency have not been adapted in any fundamental way to deal with an increasing movement of people between countries. This may result from the nature of public services, which tend to be monolithic, under-resourced and already grappling with complex social and professional situations.

The increasing layers of organisational infrastructure in modern societies may be contributing to the problem rather than the solution. The layers normally include managers, policy directors and governments. Governments and ministries decide policy and national budgets. Policy directors are responsible for the broad implementation of those policies and managers for the day-to-day implementation at a local level. Managers are subject to short-term targets and budgets against which they are appraised and rewarded; long-term policy and budgets are outside their remit. Politicians are subject to the short-term political will and priorities of the voters. The layers can become locked in a negative cycle if they become disassociated from the practical realities or when it looks as though necessary change will threaten the intricate embedded infrastructures and vested interests.

The degree of political will to confront the challenges of multilingualism varies between countries. Some countries are uninterested in, or even overtly negative towards, the welfare of individuals who do not belong to the mainstream language and culture group. Others declare themselves to be committed to the principles, but never quite get round to the practical implementation. Some, such as South Africa, have the real political will to accommodate those who speak other languages and, in particular, the eleven official languages of its own country, and are struggling to put their principles into practice with very limited resources.

Effective organisation is also needed on an international, as well as national level because of the increasing demand for international consistencies. An interesting illustration arises in the legal services of EU countries where legislation is developing to accommodate movement of people in terms of common European arrest warrants and mutual recognition of judicial decisions, bail and evidence. There is also the requirement for judicial co-operation in such matters as the prevention of terrorism and trafficking in drugs and people. None of that legislation can be reliably implemented without the relevant equivalent and internationally transparent language skills and structures. Mutual trust and judicial co-operation could both be put at risk if, for example, the French legal services could not be sure whether appropriately qualified interpreters and translators were engaged during the process of gathering evidence in England for use in a French court hearing. Similarly, could a Spanish doctor rely upon a Greek doctor's report on his patient who had been taken ill on holiday in Greece, unless complete confidence could be placed in the interpreter engaged at the hospital and the translator of the text?

The demand for interpreting skills in public services has so outstripped supply that one of the greatest obstacles to developing policies and implementation strategies is that the necessary skills and structures for the task are not available. In order to move forward, one approach would be to offer training to managers and policy makers at various levels and across the sectors such as legal, health and social services. Coherent planning, on an informed basis, has the potential to optimise the use of scarce resources; to promote systematic, incremental development of all the skill sets required and to monitor, evaluate and disseminate resulting good practice. It is worth mentioning at the outset, however, that there are two main fundamental differences between the aims of management training in the public service and commercial contexts. The first is that, while professional stewardship of resources is essential in the public service domain, professional standards of service are the primary motive rather than financial profit. This applies particularly in countries where national social infrastructures exist to supply, for example, a national health service, as in the UK and Scandinavia. Secondly, as mentioned earlier, business people are normally trained to target particular culture/language speaking groups to whom they wish to export their goods and services. In the public service sector, individuals with a range of language and cultural backgrounds can appear without warning at the doors of, say, hospitals or police stations. Therefore managers and personnel have to be trained in sound basic principles that allow their organisational framework to adapt to particular circumstances. Such training could be included in such courses as Masters in Public Administration (MPA).

What follows describes the type of tasks to be undertaken from a management point of view. Real life, however, will make it unlikely that the development of skills and structures can be done in the logical order in which they are set out. Management of change is never that tidy. But it is possible to set in place developments on an incremental basis if there is clarity, transparency and consensus over targets and processes.

Information database

It is self-evident that the first step to planning and organising a service to a multilingual, multicultural constituency is to know what that constituency consists of in terms of specific features (see points a–j below) and to store that information in a customised database for update and retrieval according to purpose. One cannot, for example, be in a position to decide how many interpreters are needed if the number of people speaking which languages is not known. The basic principle is that good service cannot be planned or given to a client group about whom not enough is known.

The information required is no more than what is needed to provide effective service and is similar to that collected for market research in commercial settings. Some relevant points need to be mentioned before considering these features. The first is to recognise that precise data are unlikely to be immediately available – a fact that deters many from even beginning to collect it. A start has to be made with rough data, which can be extended, consolidated, cross-checked and fine-tuned in the light of experience.

Existing information sources may be diverse, in need of development and of limited assistance. National censuses may or may not be helpful. The Australian census appears to be one that gives good qualitative as well as quantitative assistance in this area. The UK census currently includes a question on ethnicity, which may confuse the issue for, for example, those who have parents from different backgrounds. In the first instance, such places as schools, community centres and places of worship may be in a position to supply useful information.

Other records may also be of limited use. For example, some services may record only when interpreters or translators have been engaged and paid, but not when volunteers or family members have been used in those capacities, or indeed what languages were involved. It is also unlikely that any records will have been kept of the occasions when interpreters or translators were needed but not engaged.

It is a matter of beginning a process of information collection from a variety of reliable sources, without adding unduly to the bureaucracy. Putting in place sensible record-keeping protocols should be considered as a first step. The data collection process should also accommodate the inevitable changes over time, whereby people move between jobs, between cities and countries and develop language skills. Data collected should not encourage stereotyping but provide a backdrop to planning. Notes on individuals' relevant language and cultural preferences, including for instance, dietary preferences, can be recorded on personal files held by the relevant public service after discussion with the other-language speaker and with their agreement.

Rather than have each public service collect such data for their own purposes, it would clearly be cost and time-effective for them all to share essential core data gathering for their local area. They may then wish to add data relevant to that particular service; for example, the education service may wish to find out how many four-year olds are not fluent in the majority language in order to plan second language teaching for when the children start school at five; the health service may wish to consider if any staff in-service training is required for medical conditions specific to certain groups, such as tuberculosis (see, for example, Bakhshi, Hawker and Ali 1997).

Information gathering can feel threatening, especially for those who have fled arbitrary regimes. The process has to be carried out in ways that are consultative and transparent as to purpose. Data so collected should be accessible to both the public and to the services and not infringe the privacy of individuals or any data protection legislation. It is a matter of political debate as to whether illegal immigrants should, or can, be included within this exercise, but there are objective points to be considered in terms of health care, child protection and social factors. It should also be noted that not all illegal immigrants are transported voluntarily, as evidenced by the trafficking of sex workers, and others who have been subject to privations at the hands of people smugglers.

Once the other-language speaking public and public service staff are involved in data collection, there has to be a parallel exercise begun in the management of expectations because all that they need cannot be provided immediately. Interim information about longer-term goals and progress towards these goals can lower levels of frustration. A nationally consistent approach to data collection promotes sound planning and comparison of data between regions.

The main types of data required include:

(a) which languages other than the majority language are spoken in the area?

Language mapping is a familiar process to language specialists but not to the public services, so this is a particular example where interdisciplinary mutual support is needed. The information required concerns preferred languages according to situation of use. The database should also include information on which non-standard varieties are spoken. Mirpuri, for example, is a variety of Gujarati and Sylheti of Bengali. It is also useful to know where languages have no written form and the standards of literacy in the other languages if, for instance, translated information leaflets are being considered.

(b) how many speakers are there of each of the other languages?

Having a broad idea of the numbers involved allows planners to begin to decide on such factors as how many interpreters and translators might be needed.

(c) what is the age profile?

Age profiles have a bearing on medical and other service provision. For example, single men between 20 and 40 years of age may arrive in a new country to establish themselves in work and anticipate that their families will join them later, or three generations of a family may migrate together, or international students may be coming to attend education courses.

(d) where do the speakers of other languages live?

If there are a thousand speakers of a particular language living in one neighbourhood, it is clearly sensible to locate relevant routine language accessible facilities in that neighbourhood. Alternatives are needed where there are dispersed small groups, especially as they are often the most prone to being neglected.

(e) what form did migration take?

It is almost impossible to predict what access individuals will need to public services because anyone can suffer from appendicitis or be burgled but it is intelligent to note indicators. There is, for instance, likely to be a disparity of need arising from the mode of migration. At one end of the scale there is the individual who has had previous full access to health care and education and arrived in a country by choice, accompanied by his possessions, without risk to himself or his family and has sure housing and employment prospects. At the other end of the scale are those who have fled war, famine and extreme poverty, after years without proper health care or education and been obliged to abandon possessions and loved ones and been traumatised by both events and the journey. The former is likely to have minimal requirements. The latter's needs may be extensive, lengthy in resolution and complex.

Most fall somewhere between these extremes. Seasonal migrations include agricultural labourers and workers in the tourist industry. The former in particular provide an example of where demand on medical and other services can be minimised through the timely provision of accessible information to prevent occupational hazards and accidents.

(f) Where did the speakers of other languages come from?

It can be helpful to know which countries people originally came from and which, if any, third countries they have lived in. Individuals, who originally came from Turkey, for example, may have been 'guest workers' in Germany for some years and their children educated in German schools. Gujarati speakers may come from a rural part of Gujarat state or have spent some years in East Africa as successful traders and have a command of a range of languages. An individual's background reflects not only language skills but also familiarity with national systems. A French national used to an inquisitorial legal system for example, will need explanations on that basis if he or she comes in contact with the English adversarial legal system.

(g) What are the educational and social backgrounds of the speakers of other languages?

The standard of education of an individual can influence the likely speed of his or her acquisition of a second language and of establishment in steady and rewarding employment (Corsellis and Ferrar,

2006: 124, 158–9, 162, 171–3). On the other hand, lack of education may denote lack of opportunity particularly for women.

Some authorities have usefully invested in profiling a range of skills to provide a basis for planned development leading to self-sufficiency. People without a fluent knowledge of the majority language of the host country are likely to take jobs that, in the first instance, make limited language demands. Qualified tradesmen, such as plumbers and electricians, may find work easily where there is a shortage in these skills, as well as opportunities to formalise their qualifications in a new country. Professionals, such as doctors and lawyers, may find it harder to resume their original careers. Farmers, particularly those who had owned their own land, be it large or small, may feel its loss keenly. City dwellers may not thrive in rural communities and *vice versa*.

Religion is a significant element in some cultures. Where this is so, it has to be included in the planning information base so that appropriate provision may be made, for example, for appropriate food in hospitals and schools, places for religious observance and for accommodating likely attitudes and rituals around birth, death and bereavement.

(h) What are the projections for demographic change?

Populations are rarely static. Foreign news and immigration arrangements are useful indicators of change of both arrivals and departures. New arrivals may re-group in other areas for improved employment prospects or to be near relatives. New local factories requiring specialist international expertise, international sporting events and conferences all give rise to more predictable changes.

(i) What is the existing and projected written and spoken competence of the other-language speaker groups in the majority language?

It is not possible to quantify with any accuracy how many other-language speakers have an existing knowledge of the majority language or the speed at which they will acquire it. The length of time they have been in the country can give an indication of both language skills and understanding of national systems, but this is not always reliable. It is, however, possible to use with caution self-assessed information as to whether an individual considers he or she has a written and spoken command of the majority language which is basic, enough to manage straightforward communication or fluent. Many authorities have invested in teaching the majority language to new arrivals, allowing those who need to, to recover sufficiently from any post-migration trauma to be in a position to learn.

(j)   What do the other-language speakers see as their priority?

This question comes last but is not least in terms of significance in that other-language speakers not only need to be heard but are probably in the best position to identify and prioritise their needs. Furthermore, it enables them to gain some sense of control over their affairs and gives them an opportunity to be responsible for them.

Planning for other-language speakers cannot be done in isolation from the whole, in other words, without considering the majority community. The people who already live in a town or village, whatever their own original cultural background, have needs and perceptions too. They may feel that the newcomers threaten their own jobs, culture and way of life. Successful development work in this field accommodates new arrivals, helps the existing population to adapt to any change and support the process of absorbing newcomers.

Major cities – such as London, Paris, New York and Sydney – are used to being multicultural. Indeed they are often proud of the fact, see it as a resource and thrive on it. Places that are new to the movement of people between countries may find it more challenging and need more information, support in getting to know new neighbours and safe arenas in which to share anxieties and solve problems.

Identifying the skills needed

On the basis of the data collected, it will be clear that a range of complementary skills sets will be needed, but one also needs to know how many people with these skills are needed and where. To recap, the skills sets include:

(a)   Interpreters

How many interpreters are needed in which languages and in which geographical locations? The skills, training, qualifications and employment arrangements are described in Chapters 3, 4 and 5.

(b)   Translators

The same questions apply for interpreters.

(c)   Bilingual Staff

As these are people who possess dual skills – language and vocational – they are in a position to deliver their expertise directly to someone from a second language and cultural background. (see Chapter 6)

(d) Staff trained for work with interpreters and translators and across cultures

The skills are already described (see Chapter 7). Clearly, these staff need to be appropriately deployed.

(e) Research and development

Anecdotal evidence and apocryphal stories abound in the public services of what works, what doesn't and why in the deployment of interpreters and translators. Properly conducted research is much needed to guide policy decisions on training and operation of the services provided. A relevant background in interpreting and/or translation, project management, language-based technology, mental health care, intercultural communication and so on, is the best starting point for such research projects in order to avoid costly and unproductive outcomes. This can be achieved by a combination of permanent staff *in situ* and external experts trained in appropriate research methods. Its management will be discussed briefly later in this chapter.

Establishing structures and priority tasks

Once there is a broad understanding of what the demand on the services is likely to be (by whom and from where) and the configuration of skills sets needed to supply that demand has been identified, then consideration can be given to developing the structures to deliver the appropriate level and quality of service.

Decisions have to be made as to whether to start with one particular area of a public service or to implement change across the board. The former might be easier, but it is then difficult to justify why one hospital department has qualified interpreters, translators and bilingual practitioners and the others do not. Apart from anything else, experience has shown that interpreters find themselves being 'poached' in the hospital corridors for pressing needs in the areas without. Suggestions have been made about establishing centres of excellence from which good practice might be disseminated but that too has its drawbacks, not least the length of time needed to achieve results.

There is extensive literature on management and the management of change in particular (see, for example, Balogun and Hope Hailey, 2004; Tushman and Anderson, 2004). Much of it applies to commercial settings, but some topics, such as market research are relevant to a public services environment. The following points (i–xiii) cover some of the main elements of establishing PSI services where there are additional or different factors to be considered than in the management of other environments.

i. Team building
    Team building is always a prerequisite in any development work. There is usually a need for a series of layered and interconnected teams focusing on broader or narrower themes. The key is to keep the team dynamics alive and the work moving systematically towards clear long- and short-term goals. Members of teams have to have been selected for their expertise, not simply because of their position or their ethnicity, and each one valued for what they bring to the table. Teams should be disbanded as soon as a specific task is done and then reconstituted, probably in a different form, for another task. Individuals should be allowed time between development tasks, if they wish, so that they can use a period of different or routine work to re-energise themselves.

    Each individual member is clearly engaged not only with the particular team activity but also formally engaged through an agreed process with their own service discipline or organisation. Communication of views, ideas and decision-making therefore flows from team members to their line managers and other colleagues, as well as in the other direction. Careful consideration has to be given as to how best to do this. Otherwise, it is possible for team members, such as a police officer or a housing officer, to become very well informed and motivated about an aspect of the work and not be able to interest his or her superiors or colleagues. Individual team members should therefore be mandated to make decisions or report directly to those who can, otherwise the team's work becomes disconnected.

    Development work is a live, organic process. It differs in some aspects from, for example, straightforward business meetings in order to allow thoughts to be explored and shared and agreed on a consensual basis. Decisions can be made as to whether team gatherings should be formal minuted affairs or informal or a combination of both. Formal and informal communication between the teams, and a clear understanding of the whole by everyone, is part of the process. It takes a special sort of leadership to guide the process through.

    Experienced managers will be familiar with all these points, but two of the main differences in this field of work are these. Firstly, it is interdisciplinary. This means that the public service disciplines have to work together, for example, police, courts, education, housing, medical and social services – and, of course, interpreters and translators. There are occasions when people from the different disciplines have not had an opportunity to work together, except at specific formal levels. They have been known to use this arena as an opportunity to discuss informally a range of subjects, not directly related to the matter in hand, to great benefit. It is a matter of allowing that to happen, for it becomes part of the attraction of being involved and strengthens the group dynamic while not allowing it to get in the way of the primary purpose.

The second difference in this type of development work is that it is intercultural, not only in the sense of ethnicity discussed earlier but also in respect of the cultures of professional disciplines. This is reflected in a range of ways. The conventions of various 'discourse communities' (after Swales 1990: 23ff) i.e. professionally defined groups who communicate using specialist language vary: members of the social services and medical practitioners have different professional conventions. Decision-making and hierarchies differ between the services and have to be respected.

ii. Consultation with other-language speaking groups

Consultation with the other-language speaking groups clearly involves exchanges between people of different ethnic backgrounds and cultures. Trompenaars and Hampden-Turner, in their book *Riding the Waves of Cultures* (2001), set out the challenges of working with and across cultures for middle managers of multinational companies. He describes in broad terms different cultural approaches to such aspects as work, work-life balances, decision-making, codes of conduct, consultation and managing change. Much of this also applies to management in the public sector, especially because those involved are not highly skilled international diplomats but ordinary people seeking to negotiate solutions that are important to them.

Conventions for consultation and discourse vary between cultures. This is well known to translators, interpreters and their linguist colleagues, but not necessarily to PSEs. Different concepts of meeting structures, power structures, right to speak, punctuality, turn-taking conventions, decision-making procedures, politeness conventions, levels of directness, and so on, may lead to intercultural misunderstandings and potential breakdowns in communication which may – or may not – be apparent. A *modus vivendi* may have to be discussed overtly in order to establish a common communication framework for conducting meetings.

A workable communication framework aims to facilitate a full exchange of views involving all interested parties, not only those who act as community leaders of other-language speaker groups, but also those who, for reasons of age, gender, language or religion may otherwise be excluded. It would be presumptuous to overlook traditional hierarchies and customs but community leaders can be encouraged to collaborate in allowing other voices to be heard. Some of their concerns may arise from a desire to protect their group from powerful authorities who may, even if only out of ignorance, in their view cause harm. It is a concept that can come as a surprise to, say, health care workers who see themselves as only forces for good. Mutual trust has to be developed. Community leaders who, on the basis of their bilingual skills, have acted as interpreters may well be reluctant to abandon that role as it has given them access to information about transactions between their group and the public services, enabling them, in their view, not only to protect members of their group but also to save the group's face where necessary.

iii. Managing employment and deployment of skills sets

Comments on the employment of the different skills sets are in the chapters that deal with them. The detail will depend upon the employment laws of individual countries. Suffice it to say at this juncture that public service managers would be wise to consider the fact that reliable second language skills are at a premium in other walks of life, such as commerce. If the workplace is made unnecessarily disagreeable for interpreters and translators in the public service context, they are likely to have the choice to take employment elsewhere.

People in any discipline, who choose to work in the public services, are aware that they could usually earn higher salaries elsewhere. They choose not to do so because the public service work offers them an occupation which they see as interesting, worthwhile and stimulating. Public service interpreters and translators are no exception. Nevertheless, financial rewards should still reflect the level of professional skills and support a reasonable quality of life, on a par with colleagues in other public service professional disciplines (see Chapter 5).

In respect of deployment, it used to be (and maybe still is) a standing army joke that good cooks would be sent to mend tanks and good engineers sent to work in the kitchens. The data collection process will give an indication of where the different skills sets should be deployed. It is self-evident that interpreters, translators and public service employees with second language skills should be available according to the language needs of the public. There also needs to be a match between supply and demand in particular situations. For example, if interpreters are provided for other-language speaker parents one afternoon a week to discuss nursery school arrangements, they will find themselves interpreting on pressing matters concerning benefits and housing instead unless adequate facilities have been made for those subjects to be dealt with elsewhere.

Deployment strategies, as listed below, can be used to improve cost-effectiveness; these include grouping provision according to other-language speakers, where the numbers allow it:

- Language-specific days for multiple purposes. For example, a city council can have an interpreter on duty for a specific language on one particular morning per week. The interpreter passes on to the receptionist the nature of the matter and the appropriate local government officer, trained in how to work with an interpreter, meets with the enquirer. Where this has happened, there is some anecdotal evidence that housing stock is improving as tenants are able to report faults before extensive damage occurs. In addition, the tenants are able to feel more in control of their own affairs and therefore to take better care of their properties.
- Language-specific events for a particular purpose. Antenatal classes and examinations are a good example where it is relatively straightforward to group other-language speakers in single-language groups. This also means that the group participants are likely to share cultural starting points. The young mothers may be on their own, without their own mothers, and need much more reassurance, advice and support. One bilingual health care worker, or a culturally/ linguistically aware one working with an interpreter, is more effective and more cost-effective than an interpreter making individual visits to a range of clinics. School parents' evenings are another example of particular deployment needs. At such events, information is provided about such matters as choices of subjects to be studied by children, career options, sports and educational school trips including to other countries. The education of their children is one of the most important aspects of life for newly arrived parents. They require sufficient information to support their children and make choices, whether they are highly educated themselves or not. The school environment is a good example of where bilingual practitioners can have an important role to play, as well as interpreters.
- Language and culturally specific buildings or centres. Homes and day care centres for the elderly are a case in point. It is natural to

forget words in any language as we age. Elderly people, who have led a physically and psychologically demanding life deserve, and may need, more care and support earlier than others. There have been occasions when isolated elderly people have been found in residential homes, as is the practice in some countries, unable to communicate in the language spoken by staff and other patients. There are cross-cultural perceptions about care of the elderly, which may not always be based on fact. Northern Europeans, for example, admire Asian and African cultures for their pride in taking care of their own elders. The fact is that, much as they would like to, Asians and Africans may not be able to offer that care so easily away from extended family support or perhaps a rural life style. This adds greater stresses to all generations and to professional carers. Areas where numbers allow the provision of homes and day care centres, staffed by people with the appropriate language skills, specifically for single culture and language groups have often found them to be successful.

iv. Managing support, supervision and mentoring
     Working at the interface of cultures and languages can be demanding. It can also be isolating when, for example, there is only one bilingual receptionist or speech therapist, or when interpreters work on a freelance sessional basis or translators work from home. It is tempting, because managers do not possess the relevant language and cultural skills themselves, to leave aside the need to support, mentor and supervise those who do, and who may also not be full-time members of the established staff.

     It is simply good management practice to set up and monitor sound systems for these purposes, as for any other skills sets, and make sure that the staff responsible for them are equipped to carry them out properly and consistently. It is therefore a matter of selecting from the more experienced and appropriate individuals in the various disciplines, such as interpreters, translators and bilingual staff, and giving them the necessary additional training in how to support, mentor and supervise their colleagues. This includes all the usual strategies for such approaches as setting agreed targets in terms of tasks to be done and good practice standards to be attained, supporting individuals in achieving them, mentoring professional development, supervising and appraising professional competence regularly. Where freelance interpreters and translators are engaged through agencies under contract to public services, it may be a matter of ensuring that the agencies perform those tasks by including them, for instance, in any tender.

v. Lines of communication and accountability

Lines of communication and accountability need to be established within the public services to support sensible deployment. The lines should be vertical and horizontal; upwards to communicate appropriately with line managers, downwards with more junior members of staff and sideways with colleagues in the same and other professions. What is to be communicated and/or recorded, when, how and to whom needs to be clearly identified, known and understood in order that activities which are happening within another language are not lost from sight or record. Important information and activities may fall outside mainstream formal and informal systems if appropriate procedures are not in place.

Levels and types of responsibility are usually clearly set out in the public services, and those who hold the relevant posts are accountable for the tasks specified. Their ability to act responsibly depends in large part on the information they hold. It is often the details that are significant. The relevant data recorded in the majority language on personal files may need to be supplemented where that information is not necessarily accessible or obvious to staff who do not speak the language of the individual concerned.

Interpreters and translators working on the same matter may well share terminology with each other to promote consistency and quality. They will raise any ambiguities in the source-language text or speech with their principals because they are accountable for accuracy of transfer.

The delivery of language and related skills needs to be managed on a case-by-case basis, as individuals become involved in a series of events or with a series of public service agencies. For example, the police officer needs to communicate with the court to inform them whether an interpreter will be needed. The court needs to communicate with the doctor to inform him or her whether an interpreter will be needed for a medical report and possibly a translator.

Work with individuals needs to be drawn into the wider situation where, for example, the manager needs to know whether systems for interpreter call-out are working, and if not why, because he or she is accountable for their successful operation. Clear, known lines of communication allow information to be processed accurately, quickly and in a timely manner that allows those accountable to monitor what is happening properly and take action where necessary. Such approaches also support informed development and improvement.

vi. Monitoring and evaluation

It can appear a challenge to be able to monitor and evaluate objectively systems and activities that are taking place in a number of languages. It is nevertheless particularly important to do so in a situation where there is a greater risk of not identifying errors, of not spotting inadequate processes or of not noticing underperforming or unhappy practitioners or dissatisfied clients in a timely manner, simply because the majority language is not being used.

The tasks of monitoring and evaluation require a thorough understanding both of what should be happening and of what is happening, as well as the ability to suggest informed explanations of any gaps. The answer may be multidisciplinary teams designed to look at particular aspects, operating within consistent overarching guidelines. For example, an experienced translator, a doctor and a personnel (Human Resources) officer would be able to develop and implement a system for monitoring and evaluating medical translations for a hospital.

vii. Quality assurance

Quality Assurance (QA) follows from monitoring and evaluation in that it refers to implementing the strategies identified to assure quality of service provision, and to provide the evidence for that assurance. Many would see QA as the means by which a public service makes itself accountable. Systems such as routine tape-recording of all police investigative interviews, which already happens in some countries, provides the opportunity to monitor the quality of interpreting and evidence of any inaccuracies.

Members of the public are an integral and important part of the QA process in that they contribute their views as to how satisfactory they have found the service to be. Certainly in the UK, feedback forms are left for people to complete in such places as hospitals, although not often in languages other than English. Support may also be required where individuals have literacy difficulties.

viii. Recording and disseminating good practice

Most people who have worked in the field – either on the interpreting or the public service side – for some time are aware of many notable cases of good practice. However, these may be the results of individual efforts and are not necessarily embedded in institutional codes of conduct or guidelines. Hence, good practice may cease to be implemented once particular individuals leave the institution.

Good practice needs to be identified and tested. Once found to be sound and useful, it should be recorded accurately and concisely. Then it needs to be connected to other areas of good practice, like building a jigsaw, and disseminated. Six lines on a website are sufficient to describe useful activities that have been tried and tested, such as a dietician's recipe for a halal meat dish, a medical records officer's hints on filing under different cultural naming systems, colouring prosthetics to match skin colours or adaptations of community service orders. Everyone involved is on a sharp learning curve and nothing useful should be wasted.

ix. Budgets – planning and operating controls
Proper organisation of finances is a key tool that allows things to work. Planning service delivery across languages and cultures may demand a fresh look from first principles, rather than tinkering with an existing model. It does not necessarily mean that there will be a need for a much higher expenditure, but rather that budget heads and flows of expenditure will be different.

Precise financial projections cannot be made in the field of PSIT. No one, for example, can reliably predict how many patients, speaking which languages, will be admitted to a hospital with what illnesses.

To begin with, multidisciplinary support will be needed for forward planning, which can then be monitored and learnt from as things progress. It is not a bad thing for managers to consult over financial planning with colleagues and the wider community who, once they appreciate what is being sought, can suggest cost-effective approaches and priorities. They can also then, with understanding, back a manager who wishes to apply for additional funding if necessary.

x. Management of shortcomings
It is unlikely that all the necessary skills to operate an efficient service will be available immediately in any given situation where public services operate in a multilingual environment. Therefore, responsible strategies have to be put in place in the interim with the strict proviso that short-term compromises should never become long-term solutions.

To give an example, the situation may arise where there are no qualified interpreters in the languages required at a particular time in hospitals and police stations. The best that public service managers can do is to arrange for people with potential skills to be assessed, for the best to be selected and provided with basic instructions including codes of conduct and good practice. They then need to be supported. Most importantly, everyone involved in subsequent meetings must be informed of the unqualified status of the interpreter. Engagement arrangements should include mention of limitations and any implications for insurance arrangements. Public service personnel who have been trained to work with interpreters will be more able to accommodate those limitations by briefing the interpreters carefully before each assignment, communicating in a straightforward manner, taking things slowly and cross-checking important facts. De-briefing is important to pick up learning points.

These unqualified interpreters can then be slotted into existing training programmes, wherever possible, and learn on the job. Good supervision and sensitive mentoring, even by an interpreter from a different language group, helps prevent them giving up under the pressures if they show an aptitude and wish to continue in the job.

No one would suggest that this is the optimal solution, but sometimes there is no alternative but to make the best of available resources, while taking the greatest care to reduce risks to the service, to the public and to the unqualified interpreter.

xi. Incremental steps

As already noted in relation to 'shortcomings', it can take some time to introduce a fully operational service. Structures therefore have to be put in place to develop incremental solutions.

A three-phase approach has been found to be helpful and can be completed over three years.

- During the first phase, the organisational structure is developed including the multidisciplinary teams. The collection of information is begun for the database and long-term goals defined. Existing skills and processes are identified and tested as to whether they are fit for purpose in respect of the level and type required. Interim arrangements, with appropriate levels of insurance, are put in place to meet short-term responsibilities until what is required can be achieved. Arrangements are finalised for employment or engagement of colleagues with the different skills sets. Lastly, but importantly, arrangements are made to begin to train the trainers to produce the range of skills sets needed – that includes trainers of interpreters, translators, bilingual staff, staff who will be working with linguists and across cultures, mentors and supervisors. The trainers are the multipliers, the setters of standards and the perpetuators of consistent good practice.
- The second phase establishes an annual format of component activities which includes completion of training the trainers and assessing them. The trainers then go on to begin selecting students

for their own courses later in the year and to conduct any remedial work necessary to bring their potential students up to scratch for training. The trainers run, with support, their first courses in training interpreters, translators, bilingual staff and so forth. They enter candidates for nationally recognised examinations and encourage successful candidates to apply for professional registration where appropriate. After qualification, the individuals with the range of skills sets required can apply to enter the professional workplace. On arrival, detailed job descriptions and contracts should already have been prepared for those who are to be employed by the public services directly, and letters of agreement for the freelance sessional professionals. Deployment plans should enable them to be deployed where their particular skills are most needed. Mentoring, support and supervision systems should be ready to receive them because, inevitably, their numbers are likely to be insufficient in the first instance and they should be protected from undue workloads and encouraged to remain. Continuing professional development strategies should follow after an appropriate interval. Evaluation of the whole should be part of the process.

- The third phase begins an annual spiral of development, whereby the whole process is repeated to produce eventually the numbers of people proficient in the necessary range of skills and the quality of appropriate service delivery.

xii. Managing research and development

Research and development is an important aspect of service delivery. It supports a more detailed and objective evaluation of current practice than can be achieved by day-to-day monitoring and evaluation. More importantly, it can promote improvements in particular aspects of the services provided.

Managers may choose to engage consultants – often skilled in systems analysis, process review and statistics – to work with local staff on carefully selected projects. Some consultants specialise in the public services.

It may be better, where possible, in a development process to use internal staff for research, supported and guided by experienced researchers. Staff can then learn through involvement in the research process, through engaging with the subject at a detailed level, through negotiating ways forward, through absorbing the unquantifiable but qualitatively essential minutiae and then taking ownership of the outcomes to give them a basis of informed understanding for future development and evaluation.

Academics also have valuable contributions to make by providing rigorous and objective exploration of new approaches, as well as evaluation of current ones. Academic interests are, however, generally broader than those of the public services, where improvements to services are the prime aim of research projects; these are therefore designed to produce outcomes with immediate potential for application, such as a comparative study of different modes of interpreting – telephone, videoconference or face-to-face – in order, for example, to determine their suitability (if any) for evidential purposes. Academics may also be interested in pursuing research questions with less obvious potential for immediate exploitation, such as turn-taking in medical consultations.

As in any research project which is ethically conducted, approaches should accommodate the ethical and professional codes of the service as well as those of the academic disciplines concerned. If students are involved in such projects, for example, appropriate research training must be provided, e.g. in research design, quantitative *versus* qualitative approaches, data types, data gathering techniques and instruments, data analysis and interpretation and research ethics. Training of this kind is becoming increasingly available as an integral part of postgraduate programmes in many countries, sometimes at masters level but more often at doctoral level. Without adequate training and briefing in codes of conduct and professional practice for those carrying it out (whether students or local staff), research projects may lack objectivity and reliability, as well as wasting valuable resources such as staff time. At worst, sensitive situations could be ethically compromised.

The results of such research also need to be disseminated in ways which are accessible to decision-makers and to professionals in other disciplines. In addition to publication through the usual academic, peer-reviewed outlets, research results can also be adapted for inclusion in good practice guidelines, in-service training programmes (e.g. on DVD) or in professional journals.

For those seeking to manage research in the public service context, it is worth looking at the approaches by which scientific and IT research has been conducted and implemented by the public services over the last 50 years. These have often involved a close interdisciplinary collaboration between researchers and public service practitioners, from identification of the problem to be solved through the research process to solutions and dissemination. Cardiac pacemakers, machines that determine the level of alcohol in motorists' blood and specialist computer software have all been developed through such collaboration. As examples of applied research, based upon earlier pure research, all have tangible practical benefits.

xiii. Service delivery

There are a number of stages in the delivery of a service. The factors described above apply to them all, from gathering the database to finding out who the recipients are, through delivering the service to monitoring and maintaining its quality.

Two stages in particular are worth mentioning in more detail:

(a) Managing the provision of accessible information

An overall view is needed to put in place the solutions that can deal with the specific.

Finding a dentist to deal with a raging toothache in a country one does not know and where one does not have a fluent grasp of the language, is a challenge. One might manage if this were only a holiday experience, but if one is trying to gain access to a range of essential services as someone staying in a country for a longer time, one needs accessible information about those services and how to use them.

Reportedly, research in Birmingham, UK showed that other-language speakers held inadequate information about the essential public services they needed to use to attain quality of life and to conduct their own affairs. Furthermore, it was shown that other-language speakers often held worrying degrees of misinformation gathered second-hand. This included deaf people, who may also be excluded from the usual means of formal and informal dissemination of information about, for example, legal and health services. They were further dissuaded from approaching the services because their privacy would be compromised by having to use members of their family or language community as intermediaries to gain the information they needed. No middle-aged lady wishes to discuss her gynaecological problems with her son because he is bilingual. No young man wishes to share his anxieties about sexually transmitted diseases with a community elder. Young mothers may wish to discuss contraception, nursery provision or simply how to get to a public library without grannies or husbands interfering. Adequate and appropriate provision of information allows individuals to become independent to the degree and at the rate that suits them.

More information is needed than is normally given because other-language speakers are likely to be coming from a different starting point, that may not include the background information that it can be safely assumed that speakers of the majority language already know. Those who are born in a country, or have lived there for some years, will have an existing broad understanding of its public services. They know, for example, where to take a child with spots for medical advice, who to telephone if there is a medical emergency or a burglary, where to go for advice on housing and what a school parents' evening entails. They know, even in general terms, something about the training and qualifications of different public service professionals and about their codes of conduct. Information given to the speakers of the majority language is therefore more concerned with topping up or updating existing information. Information given to other-language speakers should accommodate their different starting points.

Information giving has to be well organised so that is an ongoing process: layered, consolidated and updated. That has to apply to both the general context and to the specific, so that a family that has been robbed can understand the relevant legal processes and the progress of the investigations and outcomes of any trial. The Victim Support systems should be as accessible to other-language speakers, who may be particularly vulnerable, as to the indigenous population. People with elderly relatives, and indeed the elderly themselves, should have an overall understanding of the facilities available to them as well as a true understanding of what is happening at each stage of care, so that they can participate in discussions and collaborate in care on an informed basis.

(b) Managing service adaptations to different cultures

Mention is made in Chapter 7 of training public service personnel in delivering a service to meet, wherever possible, the needs of individuals and their different cultural starting points. At its simplest, this means that when they have a bad cold, an Englishman may like a whisky and a Frenchman prefer a tisane. Birth and death carry their own variations between cultures and between individuals. A court's community sentence order is more likely to achieve its aim if the relevant cultural accommodations are made.

Delivery of service in these situations needs to be underpinned by planning and organisation. For example, the correct religious officials or ministers should be known and their names and contact details readily accessible, on a twenty-four hour basis, in case of death or bereavement. Dieticians and school caterers need to have their ingredients sourced and delivered. All services need quick access to translated standard forms in the range of languages they require.

The lines of communication between managers and the people who deliver various services should be close enough to allow the backup to evolve in response to the needs. Interpreters, translators and bilingual practitioners are useful sources of information about how provision might be improved for people from particular cultures and would welcome the opportunity to contribute.

Communication and accountability extends beyond the immediate context to such organisations as government departments, all the relevant professional bodies and to colleagues in other regions.

Conclusion

This concluding chapter has brought together the main strands of activity needed to deliver public services to a multilingual, multicultural constituency. Aiming to provide a preliminary orientation to the principal questions involved, it leaves more in-depth exploration to future publications.

The primary aim has been to show – in practical terms – how each one of these activities is valuable in itself but at the same time dependant on others. Qualified interpreters and translators, for example, need to work within a framework which employs, deploys and supports them. Equally, without qualified interpreters and translators, public service activities cannot function efficiently in a multilingual, multicultural environment.

Management of these strands of activity includes creating the connections between them and making them work. Implementation requires collaborations between professional disciplines, and between professional groups and local communities. Competent, practical solutions also need to be developed beyond the local level in order to work towards consistent standards at national and even international level.

Given increasing international mobility, there is a growing imperative to find solutions. There are high risks attached to doing nothing or doing it badly. Good intentions are laudable but competence, commitment and consultation are needed to realise them in practice. In the absence of effective tools, skills and strategies for the purpose, it is not only those who do not speak the language of the country that find themselves disadvantaged but also the public service employees involved, as well as the wider community.

Public service delivery almost always involves a team comprising a number of disciplines. Those teams now have to add individuals with appropriate language skills to their number and to give them the space, support and respect to become full team members. For their part, interpreters, translators and bilingual professionals are doing what they can to earn the trust of colleagues in other professions in order to deal with a new social reality.

Further suggested activities

- plot the sequence of events in a public service process and identify where a translation would be needed e.g. housing application, criminal investigation, divorce proceedings, medical consultation (minor or major)
- consider how a new immunisation programme might be organised and implemented for a multilingual, multicultural locality
- observe local public spaces, such as hospitals and schools, and see whether the information and guidance displayed would meet the needs of other language speakers in the area
- when visiting a country where you do not speak the language well, see if you can find out how you would contact the emergency services to report a fire or accident.

Further reading

Angelelli, C. V. (2004) *Medical Interpreting and Cross Cultural Communication*. England: Cambridge University Press.

Angelelli, C. V. (2004) *Revisiting the Interpreters' Role*. Amsterdam/Philadelphia: John Benjamins.

Hackett, S. and Connell, T. J. (2006) *Setting up as a translator*. City University Monograph.

Handy, C. (1995) *Beyond Certainty: The Changing World of Organisations*. London: Random House.

Erik Hertog, and B. van der Veer (eds) (2006) *Taking Stock: Research and Methodology in Community Interpreting*. Antwerp: Hogeschool Antwerpen (Hoger Instituut voor Vertalers en Tolken). Linguistica Antverpiensia, New Series 5.

Jacobs, E. A., Lauderdale, D. S., Meltzer, D., Shorey, J. H., Levinson, W., and Thisted, R. A. (2001) 'Impact of Interpreter Services on Delivery of Health Care to Limited-English-proficient Patients', *Journal of General Internal Medicine* 16(7): 468–74.

Riddick, S. (1998) Improving Access for Limited English-Speaking Consumers: A Review of Strategies in Health Care Settings. *Journal of Health Care for the Poor and Underserved* 9 (supplemental): 40–61.

Notes

1   What is All this About?

1. 'A lipspeaker has exceptionally clear speech movements. They will face the deaf person, and repeat what the speaker says, without using their voice, so that the deaf person can lipread them. The Lipspeaker uses the same rhythm and phrasing of speech as used by the speaker, and supports the message with facial expressions and natural gestures.' 'A Speech to Text Reporter (STTR) uses a special phonetic keyboard to type what is being said. This keyboard is able to produce information at very high speeds. The text is instantly displayed, either on a laptop screen, or on a larger projection screen.' (source: http://www.cacdp.org.uk/, the website of the UK-based Council for the Advancement of Communication with Deaf People (CACDP)).
2. See, for instance, *Discussion Paper 46 (2004) – Blind or deaf jurors* from the New South Wales Law Reform Commission (http://www.lawlink.nsw.gov.au/lrc.nsf/pages/dp46toc).

5   Establishing a Professional Framework

1. The concept of 'native speaker' is becoming increasingly problematic in the modern world (see, for instance, Anderman and Rogers 2005, 14–16 in relation to translation).
2. The Clementi Review on the Law Society, for example, proposes a split between the regulatory and membership structures (http://www.legal-services-review.org.uk/).

7   Responsibilities and Training of Public Service Staff

1. On rare occasions, such as in large-scale court proceedings of an international kind involving lawyers from two legal systems and languages, for instance, simultaneous interpretation from a booth (which usually has to be hired and installed for the occasion) may also be provided.
2. The principles of commissioning an interpreter have been discussed in the good practice guide in Chapter 3.

8   Management and Policy

1. See, for instance, a revised England and Wales *Agreement on Arrangements for the use of Interpreters* published in January 2007 (downloadable from http://www.police.homeoffice.gov.uk/).

References

Anderman, G. and Rogers, M. (2005) 'English in Europe: For better, for worse?', in G. Anderman and M. Rogers (eds) *In and Out of English: For Better, For Worse?* (pp. 1–26). Clevedon: Multilingual Matters.

B.B.C. *Born Abroad. An Immigration Map of Britain.* http://www.bbc.co.uk/bornabroad (site visited 11 September 2007).

Baker, C. (2000) 'Bilingualism', in M. Byram (ed.) *Routledge Encyclopedia of Language Teaching and Learning* (pp. 82–4). London and New York: Routledge.

Baker, P. and Eversley, J. (2000) *Multilingual Capital.* London: Battlebridge.

Baker, V. (2006) 'Lost for Words', *The Linguist,* 45.2, 54–5.

Bakhshi, S. S., Hawker, J. I., and Ali, S. (1997) 'The epidemiology of tuberculosis by ethnic group in Birmingham and its implications for future trends in tuberculosis in the UK', *Ethnicity and Health* 2 (3), 147–53.

Balogun, J. and Hope Hailey, V. (2004) *Exploring Strategic Change.* Prentice Hall: London.

Bobrick, B. (2001) *The Making of the English Bible.* London: Weidenfeld and Nicholson.

Braun, S. (2007) 'Interpreting in small-group bilingual videoconferences: challenges and adaptation processes', *Interpreting,* 21–46.

Brennan, M. and Brown, R. (1997) *Equality Before the Law: Deaf People's Access to Justice.* Deaf Studies Research Unit: University of Durham.

BS EN 15038:2006 *Translation services. Service requirements,* available from British Standards Institute at http://www.bsi-global.com/en/ (site visited 20 October 2007).

Bunette, L., Bastin, G., Hemlin, I., and Clarke, H. (eds) (2003) *The Critical Link 3: Interpreters in the Community.* Amsterdam/Philadelphia: John Benjamins.

Cambridge, J. (1999) 'Information loss in bilingual medical interviews through an untrained interpreter'. *The Translator* 5, 202–19.

Cambridge, J. (2005) 'The public service interpreter's face: rising to the challenge of expressing powerful emotions for others', in C. Toldedano (ed.) *Revisita Canaria de Estudios Ingleses* (pp. 141–57). Universidad de la Laguna.

Carr, S., Roberts, R., Dufour, A., and Steyn, D. (eds) (1997) *The Critical Link: Interpreters in the Community.* Amsterdam/Philadelphia: John Benjamins.

Channell, J. (2007) 'The other side of the LSP fence: Commercial language consultancy and research', in K. Ahmad and M. Rogers (eds) *Evidence-based LSP. Translation, Text and Terminology* (pp. 53–74). Bern etc.: Peter Lang.

CILT (National Centre for Languages) (2006) *National Occupational Standards in Interpreting.* http://www.cilt.org.uk/standards/NOSIrev2006glossary.pdf (site visited 11 September 2007).

Connell, Tim (2006) 'The application of new technologies to remote interpreting'. *Linguistica Antverpiensia* 5, 311–24.

Corsellis, Ann (1995) *Non-English Speakers and the English Legal System.* Institute of Criminology, University of Cambridge. Cropwood Occasional Paper no. 20.

Corsellis, Ann (2003) 'Interpreting and translation in the UK public services. The pursuit of excellence versus, and via, expediency', in G. Anderman and M. Rogers (eds) *Translation Today: Trends and Perspectives* (pp. 180–91). Clevedon: Multilingual Matters.

Corsellis, J. and Ferrar, M. (2006) *Slovenia 1945*. London: I. B. Tauris.

Corsellis, A., Cambridge, J., Glegg, N. and Robson, S. (2007) 'National Registers for Public Service Interpreters: Establishment, Maintenance and Development', in C. Wadensjö, B. Englund Dimitrova and A-L. Nilsson (eds) *The Critical Link 4: Professionalisation of Interpreting in the Community*. (pp. 139–50). Amsterdam/ Philadelphia: John Benjamins.

Council for the Advancement of Communication with Deaf People (CACDP). http://www.cacdp.org.uk/ (site visited 11 September 2007).

Delisle, J., and Woodsworth, J. (eds) (1995) *Translators through History*. Amsterdam/ Philadelphia, PA: Benjamins and UNESCO Publishing.

FitzGerald, H. (2003) *How different are we? Spoken discourse in intercultural communication*. Clevedon: Multilingual Matters.

Gillies, A. (2005) *Note-taking for Consecutive Interpreting – A Short Course*. Manchester: St. Jerome.

Hertog, E. (ed.) (2001) *Aequitas: Access to Justice Across Language and Cultures*. Antwerp: Lessius Hogeschool.

Hertog, E. (ed.) (2003) *Aequalitas. Equal Access to Justice across Language and Culture in the EU Grotius project 2001/GRP/015*. Antwerp: Lessius Hogeschool.

Hertog, E., Corsellis, A., Rasmussen, K. W., Vanden Bosch, Y., Van der Vlis, E., and Keijzer-Lambooy, H. (2007) 'From Aequitas to Acqualitas: Establishing standards in legal interpreting and translation in the European Union', in C. Wadensjö, B. E. Dimitrova and A-L. Nilsson (eds) *The Critical Link 4: Professionalisation of Interpreting in the Community* (pp. 151–66). Amsterdam/ Philadelphia: John Benjamins.

Home Office Police (2007) *Agreement on Arrangements for the use of Interpreters* http://police.homeoffice.gov.uk/news-and-publications/publication/ operational-policing/national-agreement-interpret.pdf (site visited 10 January 2008).

Ife, A. (2005) 'Intercultural Dialogue: The Challenge of Communicating across Language Boundaries', in G. Anderman and M. Rogers (eds) *In and Out of English: For better, for worse?* (pp. 286–98). Clevedon: Multilingual Matters.

Keijzer-Lambooy, H., and Gasille, W. J. (eds) (2005) *Aequilibrium: Instruments for Lifting Barriers in Intercultural Legal Proceedings*. Amsterdam: ITV Hogeschool voor Tolken en Vertalen.

Kelly, L. (1979) *The True Interpreter. A History of Translation Theory and Practice in the West*. New York: St. Martin's Press.

Kelly, N. (2007) *Telephone Interpreting: A comprehensive guide to the profession*. Clevedon: Multilingual Matters.

Márquez-Reiter, R. (2005) 'Complaint calls to a caregiver service company: the case of desahogo'. *Intercultural Pragmatics* 2.4, 481–513.

Mühleisen, S. (2002) *Creole Discourse: Exploring Prestige Formation and Change across Caribbean English-Lexicon Creoles*. Amsterdam/Philadelphia: John Benjamins.

Naming Systems published by the Judicial Studies Board in London 2005 (produced as training material for magistrates).

New South Wales Law Reform Commission (2004) *Discussion Paper 46 (2004) – Blind or deaf jurors.* http://www.lawlink.nsw.gov.au/lrc.nsf/pages/dp46toc (site visited 11 September 2007).

Ozolins, U. (2000) 'Communication Needs and Interpreting in Multilingual Settings: The International Spectrum of Response', in Roberts et al. (eds), pp. 21–35[0].

Regina v. *Endenico Belo* (2007) Computer Aided Transcript of the Stenograph Notes of Smith Bernal Wordwave Ltd. Neutral Citation Number: [2007] EWCA Crim. 374 in the Court of Appeal, Criminal Division, 9th February 2007.

Regina v. *Iqbal Begum* (1991) 93 Criminal Appeal Reports 96 9.

Roberts, R., Carr, S., Abraham, D., and Dufour, A. (eds) (2000) *The Critical Link 2: Interpreters in the Community.* Amsterdam/Philadelphia: John Benjamins.

Schellekens, P. (2001) *English as a Barrier to Employment, Education and Training.* DfES.

Swales, J. W. (1990) *Genre Analysis. English in academic and research settings.* Cambridge: Cambridge University Press.

Trompenaars, F. and Hampden-Turner, C. (2001) *Riding the Waves of Cultures.* London: Nicholas Brealey Publishing.

Tushman, M. L., and Anderson, P. (eds) (2004) *Managing Strategic Innovation and Change: A Collection of Readings.* New York: Oxford University Press.

van der Vlis, E-J. (2003) 'Implementing a Model: The Dutch Experience', in E. Hertog (ed.) (2003) (pp. 149–67).

Wadensjö, C., Englund Dimitrova, B., and Nilsson, A. L. (eds) (2007) *The Critical Link 4: Professionalisation of Interpreting in the Community.* Amsterdam/Philadelphia: John Benjamins.

Index